PREFACE

Even if you've never sold anything online before, this guide will assist in building your confidence, growing your knowledge and most importantly, hopefully increasing your income while doing something you love. This is not a step-by-step guide, because you can find those instructions anywhere. This book is different, and is meant to tell you the things that aren't mentioned in other places, such as useful information on sourcing, shipping and research. Included are time-saving customer service communications samples you can customize throughout. One of the biggest fears I hear from people relate to the nightmare stories of scammers or bad buyers. I address this (very rare) occurrence and provide tried and true tips to protect your profits and avoid problem buyers.

Although geared towards the Beginner, there is information that even seasoned sellers may find helpful when it comes to protecting yourself and in using diplomacy when dealing with difficult customers.

I have shared this information over the years in bits and pieces with reseller groups online and have assisted multiple friends in getting their business started to supplement or replace their income, or even just thin down their collections. People consistently tell me how helpful the hints are, so I have consolidated them into an easy-to-read book with a humorous (and possibly offensive) slant at times…after all, my background is construction. I hope you enjoy the book as much as you will enjoy your new adventure of learning to sell online.

Copyright 2024 – Neon Press
All Rights Reserved

ISBN: **9798321217245**

EBAY FOR BEGINNERS:

Overcoming Fear and Finding Success

Everything You Need to Know to Build Confidence and List That First Item!

Learn Tips About Sourcing, Research and Shipping, as Well as How to Avoid the Scammers and Master Customer Service

Copyright © 2024   Neon Press
All rights reserved.

DEDICATION

This book is dedicated to the two most important men in my life:

My Husband, who not only shares in the enjoyment of the hunt and has considerable knowledge of his own, but has most importantly, never hesitated to support me in every aspect, and has been beside me as my best friend and partner every step of the way in not only the pursuit, but also the achievement of my dreams of doing what I love as a career.

Also, my Father, who taught me the thrill of the hunt and instilled both the love and the knowledge required to pursue my dreams. You always told me that if you do what you love as a career, that you will never work a day in your life. I wish I had listened to you much earlier, and know you're looking down at me and smiling at the results of your teachings.

DISCLAIMER

Much of the information in this book is subject to change over time. Online marketplaces often change their policies. Shippers, PayPal, postal service, etc., also update their policies on a regular basis. The book is meant to be a general guideline, so please double check on your own for any changes that may have occurred, which could impact how you handle your online sales business, as info may have changed since the writing of this book.

CONTENTS

1	What do You Know and Love?	6
2	Where do I Sell?	9
3	Where do I Find Stuff to Sell?	17
4	What do I Need to Get Started?	23
5	The Importance of Good Research	29
6	The "EBay Mentality" and "Antiques Roadshow Syndrome"	35
7	Beg, Borrow & Steal (Nightmare Buyers)	46
8	The Art of Diplomacy (aka, "Being Able to Tell Someone to Go to Hell and Making Them Look Forward to the Trip")	70
9	Packaging and Shipping or "The Space and Time (and Cost) Continuum"	83
10	FedEx and UPS Surprise Charges – Planning and Avoiding Extra "Dimensional Weight" Costs	94
11	Accounting/Record Keeping	98
12	Quick Reference – The 10 Most Common Questions and how to Address Them	101
	About the Author	115

CHAPTER 1
What Do You Know and Love?

Step 1 in any business is figuring out what you know best and what you love to do. You wouldn't marry someone you don't know and love (well, most of you wouldn't), so don't marry yourself to a business that you won't enjoy. Otherwise, just like a weekend fling marriage in Vegas…it's going to fail and probably cost you a lot of money in the long run.

Perhaps your passion is vintage toys or electronics; maybe you love jewelry. Do you know everything about Fenton glassware? Are you in tune with the brands of kid's clothing that sells? Use that knowledge as a main focus. Where it is certainly not a necessity, nor perhaps even be possible to limit yourself to only one area of expertise when it comes to selling, it is much easier to get started if you choose something in an area where you have a base knowledge. If you don't have a particular passion, that's OK, too, but a strong knowledge about what you are listing is a big plus until you get the hang of extensive keyword search terms and exactly what to say to attract buyers.

My biggest area of knowledge is probably art pottery and vintage glassware. I find that I very often have an advantage over other buyers at auctions and estate sales because I know about these items. I can spot a piece of Moorcroft pottery across a room and almost instantly tell you if a particular piece of glass is Blenko by the color/form. Just recently, I found a piece of misidentified pottery at auction. The auction house had it listed as Weller pottery. It wasn't marked, and when I previewed the auction, I recognized the glaze and form as unmarked old Roseville pottery, which is worth about 4 times what a similar piece of Weller would sell for. That is where your knowledge will give you an advantage. There's an old adage that says "you make your money when you buy, not when you sell", and you will find that to be true. I was willing to pay much more than everyone else at the auction for that piece, because I knew it was a potential $300-$400 sale, not a $75-$100 piece of pottery.

As you advance in learning how to list items and you get a feel for your supply sources (we will talk about supply sources in a future chapter), it will make it easier to expand your knowledge base while subsequently expanding the variety of items you are comfortable in selling. Although I love pottery & glass, it is impossible for me to buy and sell only those items, simply because there isn't enough available to make it a viable business. Outside of those areas, I know a little about a lot of things, and nothing about many. That's where the miraculous invention (thanks, Al Gore) of the internet comes in. There is a wealth of information out there for research and you will find that your research skills will improve with every item you obtain.

You can start selling online with little or no money. Almost everyone has something they collect, and getting started will go much faster if you have a collection that has gotten out of hand, or have duplicate pieces in your personal collection and want to downsize. My first experience in selling was getting rid of some old household and decorative items I no longer needed. I basically had an online yard sale. That online sale provided about $250 in starting capital. Think about what you have that you would like to liquidate, or think about an area you would like to concentrate on. We will discuss setting up your seller accounts and basic supplies to get you started on your first sale in the next chapter. You will find that you probably already have 95% of what you need to start on hand.

As you search for that first item to sell, keep in mind the size and weight. You don't want to list a dresser and then wonder how you're going to package and ship it. "Smaller than a bread box" is a good rule if you have to ship. Obviously, if you are selling on local marketplace, then let the buyer worry about loading it and getting it home. I would also suggest not picking something that has a high value or would be extremely fragile to ship unless you have experience in prior online selling. You don't want to end up being disappointed or discouraged on your first listing. The first item you list shouldn't be something where you are looking to make a $100 profit....just find something to get your feet wet before diving in head first. Find something you no longer want or need and won't mind if it sells for under $10. This also helps build your feedback rating if your chosen marketplace has one.

Happy Hunting!

CHAPTER 2
Where Do I Sell?

Making a decision about where to sell your items can seem to be a bit of a daunting task. "What do I need to know?", "What are the risks?". "I've heard nightmare stories about eBay transactions!". "I know nothing about how to create a listing.".

I'm not going to go into the mechanics or step by step instructions of how to fill out your information on sales platforms. That information is readily available through each venue's individual website or by watching instructional videos online. Instead, this is meant to be a guide of what I have found works or doesn't work with different seller sites. Risks and associated issues with each will be addressed in a future chapter as we get into more detailed info. 95% of my selling experience is via eBay. I have tried and successfully used other venues, but for the purpose of this book, eBay will be the main focus.

EBAY:

Hands down, this is my favorite venue for selling. You have tens of millions of built-in customers from around the world, who find your item because they are specifically looking for it. It's great for items that are easily packaged (smaller than a breadbox and light enough to easily handle on my own is my normal rule).

A seller account with eBay is free to set up. If you already have an eBay buyer account, you can sell under that ID, as well. The benefit of doing that will be that you most likely already have feedback. A zero feedback seller is sometimes looked at as an unknown and it can be difficult to make your first sale. You can change your ID name without losing your feedback if you prefer to more accurately reflect a name for a seller or your business. You probably don't want "PartyDude69" as a seller name. If you do not already have an eBay account, there are tutorials available on eBay's website or several can be found on YouTube on setting one up.

Pros:

- Big customer base.
- Relatively easy to use with templates that you fill in.
- Many options offered for your specific level of selling, ranging to meet the needs of the occasional one-item seller, or the "I sell 50,000 of the same items every month seller".
- Flexible options, allowing you to either ask a specific price, or auction to the highest bidder.
- Huge database of previously sold items that allow you to see prices you may expect to get.
- Relatively low listing costs and fees. The fee structure is available on the eBay website, but is basically 40

cents plus 10%-15% of sales price, with "store" discounts available once you reach that level.
- Multiple tutorials on both the eBay site, as well as on YouTube to walk you through step-by-step.
- Choices for payment processing and payout structure and eBay can handle processing if you do not have another source you want to use.

Cons:

- EBay is "pro-buyer". Sellers often end up on the short end of a deal if a problem arises.
- Expectations of performance. You are expected to fulfill the terms you set, such as shipping within a certain time frame, honoring a return policy, etc. If your terms say you ship within 1 day, it doesn't matter if you wake up sick; you still need to ship, and are penalized and could lose your seller account if you do not perform and fall below their standards. There is no excuse, including injury or death that will waive that requirement.
- You are never as well prepared and will never be smarter than some people are dumb. As an example, a $300 Lalique Crystal perfume bottle full of 50 year old Nina Ricci perfume, is worth that amount as a collectible because it is full and sealed. It was opened by an elderly woman who received it as a gift from the son who purchased it, then complained that the perfume was bad. Yes....it's 50 year old perfume....not 50 year old Brandy! You may naturally assume that someone would not spend $300 on perfume that they could buy for $50 for use, but they did, and I ended up with a return and refund and now had an item that lost significant value because it was opened and learned to include a disclaimer.
- There are scam artists on eBay who buy things, and then return an empty box, or a rock in a box, or who

remove parts they need from items and then return. EBay forces refunds if the buyer states that an item is "not as described", so it's important to correctly describe and be truthful about condition. I tend to be overly critical in my descriptions, so buyers are happier than they expected to be. You can choose to fight a buyer and if you have great documentation, multiple photos, etc., you can sometimes win a case with eBay, but as I said before, eBay is pro-buyer and the results of most "dispute" cases will end to their benefit. No one wants to sell a $300 bracelet and get back a rock, and then have to pay the buyer for stealing it from you. Things like that can and do happen if you don't protect yourself. If you offer free returns on eBay, then you are somewhat protected, as you cannot have negative feedback left, and free returns afford you the opportunity to withhold half the value of the item if it's received back in a different condition than when shipped. Don't let these extremely rare instances dissuade you from your venture. These buyers are very rarely encountered, and somewhat depends on what you are selling. Things like video games are much more likely to be used as "free replacements" or parts for repairs than say, glassware, with you getting back a buyer's non-working game.. After over 20 years of selling, I have only had one person who tried to return a fake Dior purse in place of the real one I sold. I will get more into ways of protecting yourself BEFORE the sale occurs that discourage this behavior and the bad buyers in a future chapter.

- Large Items are sometimes prohibitive unless you have a good shipping source. Handling & shipping, as well as even being able to calculate shipping costs for large, heavy items is difficult.
- Ever-changing rules and updates. Check for seller updates every 6 months.

ETSY:

Etsy was originally set up as a marketplace for hand-made goods and crafts. That is still the main focus, but they also allow for vintage items that are more than 20 years old. Account set up is free.

Pros:

- Low fees – 20 cents listing fee (charged every 4 months on each item) and only 6.5% fee on final sales price. They also charge a payment processing charge of 3% plus 25 cents..
- No need for outside payment processor. Etsy can handle all payment processing, collection & deposit into your account for you.
- Customer support if you have a question.
- Large customer base.
- Online tutorials to get you started on both the Etsy site and on You Tube.
- More seller friendly than eBay.

Cons:

- You can't sell everything on Etsy. Items must be 20+ years old for the vintage category and handmade items are required to have been created by you.
- Once an item is sold on Etsy, the history of the price recognized is not easy to access. You can search for items, but to see a "sold" value, you have to access each and every separate item and click in the white

space next to the listing, where the price will appear. You can easily see what others are asking for similar items, but as you will find out, asking price is one thing…..what you can actually recognize as a selling price, is another. You can also choose to pay for a sales history website membership, such as Worth Point, to determine sales history prices, but that's an expense that may or may not be worth the cost to you.

- Funds are disbursed to you only twice a month, and then funds are available based on your banking policies.

CRAIGSLIST/FACEBOOK MARKETPLACE:

We have all heard the horror stories about selling/buying on local live Marketplace sites. I have been using Craigslist for both buying & selling for about 15 years and have never had an issue. I also use Facebook Marketplace for larger items that I do not want to ship, and have also never experienced an issue. Common sense is the key. Never let a buyer into your home. I will also never set up a meeting via text only. I always call the person and get an idea of who I am talking to and check out online profile if available. Always trust your gut and do not complete a sale if you are not comfortable for any reason. Meet the person in the police station's parking lot. Many police stations now have safe exchange zones. I have used the police station on every transaction that involved electronics, as that seems to be a high risk category and if you can't check contents/working condition, don't buy it. A criminal is not going to agree to show up at the police station, and your buyer will feel much more comfortable meeting there, as well…after all, they don't know you, either. I have also sold from my storage unit facility when I had one. It was gated, with a key-code access to get in and to leave, with security cameras all around, and the criminal can't get out easily.

Pros:

- Most are free to list and free to sell – no listing fee, no transaction fees. If you sell something for $100, you get $100 if you run a cash only business.

- Cash business/immediate funds. You can choose to receive online payments, but that can be risky.

- Easy to list. Short description, few pictures, you're done.

- No shipping – buyers are all local unless you choose otherwise.

Cons:

- You are meeting strangers in person.
- Flaky people. Potential buyers call, message or text, then they don't show at times. Always have them text when they are on their way before leaving home to meet them to save yourself time and gas.
- Everyone wants a bargain. You will get low ball offers and people will ask if you can take less once you go to the trouble of meeting them. You can normally stand firm if they don't negotiate before actually meeting you. The fact that they showed up is enough to know that they're typically willing to pay full price unless condition becomes an issue. Build a little wiggle room into your price.

- Spam/Scammers. You are giving out your phone number, and although Craigslist uses a mail relay system, if you answer an email, they get your real email, as well. I don't answer emails, period, because they are typically spam. You will get spam/scam text messages, too, and when you respond, they will tell you they are out of town and want to send a money order and have an agent pick up the item. Sometimes, they want to send a money order for $300 for a $200 item and have you pay their agent. Just say "no". In person, cash only deals is the only way to avoid scams.

Other venues

Amazon, PoshMark, Letgo, OfferUp, Shopify, Bonanza, and a myriad of countless other online sites, etc. I have used Amazon a few times, but for my items, it isn't worth it. It is a very slow process to get your funds, difficult to list, expensive for fees, very restrictive for some categories, and completely buyer-friendly. I'm sure many are similar to Craigslist, but I have never used them. Shopify is more of a store-front online and I haven't tried it. They are successful venues for a reason, but I don't have enough experience to address or recommend. If you plan to buy new items for resale in bulk, then by all means, give Amazon a try. It's one listing and you can sell multiples. For me, where I rarely have more than one of any particular item, and since my items tend to be one-offs, it just doesn't make sense.

CHAPTER 3
Where do I find Stuff to Sell?

Finding items to sell is probably the most time consuming, but the most fun part of selling online. There are no "tried and true" instructions to pass along for finding items, because availability and what your geographic area offers will vary greatly. My favorite is auctions because I hate to shop....yes, a woman who hates to shop. I'll give a few ideas below of places to find items for resell, but ultimately, your choice of supply resources will depend on what you like to do, how much time you want to invest, and what is available in your area.

Auctions

Local auctions are a great supply resource for items to resell. Not all auctions are the high end auctions you see on television. Estate auctions liquidate the property of people going through bankruptcy, or sell items from the estate of people who have passed away. They also will liquidate household items, antique collections, collectibles, etc. for people looking to clean out or downsize, so they are a great resource to see a wide variety of items. I love them because I get to preview everything and do research ahead of time, which allows me to know exactly what kind of money the item will bring. I always tell people that it's like having a personal shopper who presents you with stuff that you had no idea that you needed. It's the lazy person's method of shopping, so it's perfect for me.

Auctions can be hit or miss...some weeks there is absolutely nothing, other weeks, I could easily spend $2000. You are competing with others who may be doing the same thing as you, and it's easy to get caught up in a bidding war if you have a competitive personality. Most of the auctions I buy from are online, and I will preview in person, if possible, then sit in the comfort of my own office and bid from home. If a live preview is not available, make sure you reach out to ask specific questions regarding condition, whether new or used, open box new, or if parts are missing. Most auctions are "as is where as" condition, meaning you take the risk of condition. A few auctions will offer returns if something is missing parts, damaged, or doesn't work. Check carefully so you know what your options are if you end up with something broken that wasn't disclosed. Bidding online helps take out the competitive nature of seeing the other people bid, and also keeps your competition from knowing what you buy and following your bids. Once people at my local auctions began to hear how much I made on some items and began finding me on eBay by the items I was purchasing, I began to have other resellers bid against me, taking advantage of my knowledge and the work I put into research...especially after I scored a real Salvador Dali for $125 that ended up being appraised for $4000-$6000. Those scores are the rare hits, but they are out there. My online bids are anonymous to other buyers.

Live auctions are quickly becoming a thing of the past, but if you've never been to an auction and have the opportunity to do so, it's a lot of fun. It feels a little intimidating the first time you raise your bid card, but you will become comfortable with it in no time. Remember that auctions charge sales tax and typically a 10-25% buyer's premium (you could end up paying up to 35% more than the hammer price when sold), so keep that in mind when setting a price you are willing to pay. As an example, if I purchase something that has a history of selling for $200 on eBay, and pay $100 for it at auction. My auction invoice total is typically $118, because I have a tax resell license for my state, which eliminates your need for paying sales tax on items for resell. If I then sell it for $200, eBay keeps about $26 as their commission and I use $5.00 in shipping supplies, so my actual profit is $51, not $100, and that doesn't even consider your time/gas/income tax. Make sure you take ALL costs into consideration when you are deciding what to pay for an item that you plan to resell. This is probably the biggest mistake new sellers make. Also remember that it takes the same amount of time to list an item that will yield a $7.00 profit as it does to list one that will yield a $100 profit, so make good use of your time unless you find a box of 500 $7.00 profit items that only requires the time for one listing.

You may think you can get around paying income tax, but a new law requires online marketplace payment processors to issue a 1099 form on any sales for the year that total more than $600 on their platform. You will have to count that as income, and the IRS may consider you to be a business, meaning you have to pay self-employment tax.. You may think that cash sales made in person can be hidden, but that same law instructs banks to report cash deposits over that threshold as well. If you deposit cash on a regular basis that typically exceeds your "real job" income, that could very easily catch up with you.

There are three major websites for finding auctions near you by simply entering your zip code; auctionzip.com, hibid.com and proxibid.com. Do a google search, as well. Not all auctions sell using an online auction format, so you will miss out on the places where you get the best deals. When items aren't offered online, the audience is smaller and it results in items selling for less in most cases.

Estate Sales

I've picked up a few things from Estate Sales where I have recognized good profits. It's impossible for Estate Sale companies to know everything about everything, so you can find some bargains. I find they are overpriced for resell in many cases, but if you visit the last 2 hours of the last day, you can make an offer at a fraction of the marked price and end up with some bargains. You can also find these sales and preview online in many cases by visiting estatesales.net and entering your zip code.

Garage Sales

If a seller advertises their garage sale online, you can get an idea of what is offered from their listing, which includes photos many times. There are always huge scores that you hear about from garage sales, but my overall experience with them is that you kiss a lot of frogs before you find one that turns into a prince. However, if you love garage sales and go anyway, then checking resell prices is only a few clicks away on your smartphone. There are multiple phone apps that will help you find and organize your garage sale route.

Thrift Stores

I, personally, have found very little at thrift stores for resell. However, again, it's because I'm a lazy seller. I spend bigger money to make bigger profits and sell fewer items than many online sellers. For me, my general rule is that I won't buy something if I can't make $50 on it, or it isn't worth my time to list and ship). There are people who make a living on eBay almost solely from thrift store finds. Vintage t-shirts, Hawaiian shirts, kid's clothing, designer brands, collector plates, glassware, china, etc., will all sell, and if you can list quickly, it's very easy to find $3 items that you can sell for $20-$25 all day long. Lower priced items are typically fast movers on eBay, too. Not everyone has $400 to spend for a single item, but almost everyone will spend $20 or $25 on something they want. You will sell more items, but will also have to invest more time in listing and shipping. I've lucked into a couple of good items in the past, but I don't see the value of my time in visiting multiple stores, multiple times a week to make it a viable source for me.

EBay/Marketplace

Yep, you can buy on eBay and sell on eBay or buy on various other marketplaces for resale. You can also buy on eBay and sell at live auction once you learn what tends to sell for more "live" than online. People misidentify things. I'm guilty of it myself and you will be, too. I bought a first edition Dr. Seuss book at a garage sale for a quarter, sold it for $80 and thought I had done very well. However, the person who bought it was a book expert, and recognized it as a "True" first edition, advertised it properly and sold it for almost $400. He made money buying from and then selling on eBay. I also sold a taxidermy mount, and the buyer of it reconditioned, repaired it and resold it for $200 more than he bought it for. People misspell things, they misidentify glassware/pottery, and they sell entire groupings of clothing that you could potentially separate and resell for more.

<u>Friends/Family</u>

You can actually start selling without any investment at all. Perhaps your friends have items they want to liquidate. You can consign the items, sell and keep a percentage what it sells for (I generally charge 50% of profit after all costs because it's my time and risk and I'm providing shipping materials). It's easier on them than holding a garage sale and you get pure profit. It's a bit of a risk, though, because as mentioned in a previous chapter, eBay is very buyer friendly. If you sell something, and it gets returned to you, and you have already paid your consignor, then it's you who refunds the buyer. You may even get hit with the cost of return shipping if claimed as "not as described". You also want to be careful about the expectations of your friends and family for the real value of their item(s). Someone who has paid $50 each for a collector plate may be very disappointed to learn that it only sells for $12, and after costs,, they get $4.50. Look at completed items on eBay (not listed prices, but actual prices for items that have sold), and provide a general idea of what your consignor may expect prior to agreeing to list. People almost always think their collection is worth more than it is.

You will learn very quickly, that despite where you find items for resell, that there is a big difference between prices of items based on the condition. Purses that are new, with the tag attached may sell for 90% of store retail on eBay, where the same purse, without the tag is worth only 60% of retail, and a used example may only bring 10-20% of retail.

One of the positives of buying & reselling is that it really makes you less focused on "things" in your life. When you begin to see people's lifelong collections and their possessions being sold for pennies on the dollar, you realize that your "stuff" is just....well..."stuff", and you then realize that once it's no longer "new", it's generally worth less than half what you paid. I own only a few things that I would attempt to grab if a fire broke out in my home (other than my husband and pets, of course), and those items are ones with sentimental value, not monetary value. It may also ruin you for retail shopping. Everything will begin to look overpriced to you. I would venture a guess that after doing this for years, only about 10% of my total possessions were bought new, and most of those are electronics, shoes and underwear....there are just some things you don't buy "used".

CHAPTER 4
What Do I Need to Get Started?

Other than the obvious need of a computer/smart phone and internet, your costs for getting started with selling online can vary, depending on what you want to sell. If you are going to specialize in jewelry, you will most likely need some fairly expensive equipment, like a very good camera for close up detailed photos, gemstone tester, gold testing equipment, display props, etc. I sell jewelry mixed in with multiple other items, and haven't bothered with expensive equipment. I have found that I am able to get fairly good pictures with my cell phone camera. Yes, the only camera I use is my cell phone. I do have a chemical gold/silver testing kit (about $15), and a portable diamond tester (also about $15). I also ordered basic jewelry displays for a necklace, bracelet, and ring sizer for another $10 for photography display purposes.
I only guarantee authenticity of diamonds and gold, and do not expand on synthetic vs natural, grading of stones, etc., so this works for me. If you specialize in jewelry, you will need more detailed info on a regular basis, and the equipment needed may cost you hundreds. On very special pieces, where I feel the cost is warranted, I may have a professional appraisal done. eBay's rules regarding various items changes on a regular basis, so assure that you are following their rules for any specific category, especially jewelry & high-end brand names.

For most sellers, these are the basic needs for getting started:

Camera or Cell phone with camera that is capable of clear, close up photos.

Your photography skills will be one an important aspect of selling. You need to be able to take clear photos that will show the detail necessary, and show items as small as tiny writing on the items you are selling.

This is an example of the detail I can capture with my smart phone and that technology is constantly improving.

With a little practice and using the camera features and editing capabilities on devices, you will most likely be able to sell without investing in an expensive camera. There are also multiple free online photo editing software programs that you may want to explore. Photography will end up being one of the most time consuming parts of selling online. You want to be able to get good photos with the minimum amount of time invested, so this will be an area where trial and error will help determine any additional equipment you may need.

Packing Supplies.

One of the most expensive parts of selling will be your packaging supplies. Boxes, bubble wrap, packing paper, peanuts, Styrofoam, Tape, etc. 95% of the items I sell can be shipped with nothing more than bubble wrap & packing paper & tape. Some heavy, fragile items or items with glass, such as framed art, etc., will require better protection, such as foam corners, Styrofoam, double boxing, etc. If you choose to ship USPS Priority mail, there is a wide variety of free boxes available on usps.com. Yep, completely free to use with Priority shipping only. You cannot use them for FedEx, UPS or Ground Shipments. I ship about 70% of what I sell using Priority Mail for this reason, especially smaller high-value items. I could ship a little cheaper using Parcel Post or FedEx at times, but then I would feel the need to charge the buyer for boxes within my pricing of the item, which can cost $2-$4 each. When I do buy boxes, I use U-Haul for most of my needs, and recycle boxes I receive from personal orders. I try not to ship anything larger than I can easily handle, and most of the boxes I use range from $1.00 – $4.00 each.

Postal Scale.

When listing, you will be asked to give weight and dimensions of a boxed item. Don't guess, or you will lose money on postage. Invest in a scale and weigh the item. The scale will pay for itself with just a few transactions if you're shorting yourself on postage. USPS does offer flat rate shipping for items that will fit into their flat rate box options. I use a lot of small flat rate boxes and flat rate envelopes, so weight doesn't matter. Otherwise, you will learn over time about how much to add for the weight of a box and appropriate packing material. Small items (less than 12" square) typically add up to 1 pound to weight; if larger, I add 2 pounds. Really large or heavy items, I add about 3-4 pounds to the weight of the item to assure postage is covered. I bought a postal scale that weighs up to 50 pounds from eBay for about $18.

Tape Measure/Scissors/Tape.

I found that attaching a yard stick to the edge of my packaging table and tying my scissors to a string, also attached, has saved me a ton of time. It makes life easy to measure items when listing for description, and also for a quick measure of box size when shipping without searching. I also use manual tape dispenser for packaging tape.

An area to photograph items.

I began by taking photos on my kitchen countertop, where I had good lighting. I used a white sheet, or black piece of material taped to my upper cabinets (you will find that different items photograph better on different color backdrops). After a while, I invested about $50 into a 2' square photography light box and some backdrop material. You don't necessarily need this when starting, but I have found that it makes photographs much better and eliminates reflections and clutter that can detract from your photos.

Space

This is your most difficult and most necessary commodity of all. Selling online takes up more space than you can imagine. Storage of boxes, rolls of bubble wrap, inventory, etc., requires space. I am lucky to have a 500 sf dedicated "eBay Space" in my home. If you have a dedicated space, perhaps a spare bedroom, a basement, or even your garage, you will find you can be more organized and more productive. Space constraints will make you spend more time than you should setting up and then folding and storing photography and shipping supplies, as well as trying to find stored inventory.

This is the basic set up I use in my home (I can't believe I'm showing this always messy area of my home). Since I do this full time, I typically keep more inventory than most, but having storage racks, a packaging table and space for shipping supplies is a must for my purposes. You may find that if you choose small items, you may only need to dedicate a closet space.

That's it...short list. You will be able to determine what other supplies you may find to be helpful as you progress, and can add them as necessary.

CHAPTER 5
The Importance of Good Research

The most important aspect of buying & selling for profit will be the time and effort you put into researching and properly listing an item. I know that when I look at listings, I find myself wondering how these sellers know so much about certain items. Very rarely is the answer going to be that they are an expert in a particular field....it's simply a result of good research, and good research can not only be impressive, but it will help you sell your item for top dollar.

INTERNET VS. BOOKS

The internet has made research a hundred times easier than it was even 20 years ago. I can remember when very little information was available on the internet and most information was found in books only. I am in awe of my Father, who ran an Antiques Business in a time before internet access. Every bit of his knowledge was from books and interaction with others, and he probably forgot more information in his lifetime than I currently know, despite the internet.

One particular piece that I put hours upon hours into researching in the early internet days, was an antique hand painted miniature porcelain painting of several people in period clothing that was very detailed and looked to be very well executed. It was signed with a very small signature in the bottom corner, which took a magnifying glass to see. I was able to make out "A. Ritt". That was all I needed to begin a search on miniature portrait artists who may be famous or "known". Long story short, the name search led to a result of that particular artist being the Court Painter for Catherine the Great, which then led to realizing that she was one of the people in the portrait! I paid $70 for it at auction and despite a large crack, it sold for $700 because of my research. Had it not been cracked, it would have been a very important 250 year old, $7000 piece (there's that "condition" thing again). A few hours of research, instead of taking the easy way out and simply listing as an "Antique Miniature Ivory – Detailed – Damaged", landed me probably $500 additional profit.

General Google searches, specialty Facebook collector pages, specific collector society pages, and the ever important "google image search" will be your best friends. Just a word of warning….do your own research until you have exhausted all leads before you take advantage of Facebook specialty collector page and/or collector society pages. Those folks are not there to be your assistants and should be an absolute last resort for identification. Most don't mind showing off their knowledge and identification skills to help an individual, but get really upset if you use them to make money and you will get kicked out of groups if you abuse the gracious help they provide. Be honest with them, say please and thank you and let them know you have exhausted leads. Keep in mind that if you rely on others too much, you could get bad information, and even worse, you will never build the knowledge base that is only gained through personal research.

I will also warn that there are details on items that can make one item worth much more than another seemingly identical item. One number off in the model number...perhaps a rare color, etc., can turn what you thought was a $100 profit into a loss very quickly. On the other hand, it can turn what you thought was a $100 profit into a much larger one if the research goes your way. Look at details very carefully when researching and don't automatically assume that what you first find online matches what you have.

Some books are still important to own, especially if you decide to specialize in a particular area. I tend to buy a lot of porcelain and pottery, and a book that I could not live without is a book of antique pottery and porcelain marks. As the internet continues with the ever-increasing expansion of available information, the need for physical books may diminish, but a specialty book on "Westmoreland Glass" is always going to verify identification more easily than searching "Westmoreland Glass" on the internet and sorting through the thousands of other pieces that people may own...and who may have it misidentified, which brings me to my next point.

USING OTHER PEOPLES' RESEARCH:

Don't trust what other people have researched and listed. The identification of an item is only as good as the person who researched, and let's face it...people on the internet who argue over cat memes are not always the best choice of people to trust when it comes to knowledge. I found one item (glassware) that at least 7 different people had identified incorrectly on eBay. I'm sure one person listed it with bad information, then another person found that listing, copied the research, and so on and so on and so on. I call it the "Faberge' Organics shampoo effect". You will only understand that reference if you are of a certain age. Otherwise, you may have to research it.

The problem was not only that several people had it wrong, but had they correctly identified it, they could have sold it for 3 times the amount. eBay is a great research tool for information, but make sure you check multiple sources before you list something incorrectly. Incorrect information can result in a "not as described" claim from your buyer on eBay, which will result in you having to pay to have the item returned to you, as well as fully refunding the buyer what they paid for the item and original postage and may receive bad feedback, as well. As you progress, you will realize that eBay is full of misidentified items. Be better than those sellers.

On the other side of the coin, I listed some Tiki Mugs that came from the famous Las Vegas restaurant, Aku Aku, which opened inside the now demolished Stardust Hotel/Casino in 1960. These particular mugs were available in lots of different tourist locations across the world in the 1960s. However, I knew they were from the Aku Aku because the estate I purchased them from was that of a gentleman who worked there for decades, and were part of an Aku Aku mug collection. I listed them for about $40 more each than the typical same mug that did not have that history. Immediately, other sellers changed their description to match mine, because I was getting so much more for my pieces. However, theirs were almost certainly NOT from Aku Aku. They did not bother reading the provenance statement in my listing, so their items were misidentified.

RESEARCH BEFORE AND AFTER THE PURCHASE:

Your most important research will take place PRIOR to purchasing an item for resell. I preview every auction either online or in person and will rarely buy something I haven't thoroughly researched or already have vast knowledge on. Buying used items for resale from most auctions does not generally allow the opportunity to return items to the place of purchase if you discover an issue afterwards, so if you make a mistake, or miss seeing damage because you didn't inspect the item or ask questions, it will cost you. Most auction houses will disclose if something is damaged, but they handle thousands of items weekly and can't be expected to see a tiny chip on the bottom of a baccarat wine glass that will cut the resale value of the piece by more than 50%.

I buy many things that I know very little about, but I research them and learn as much as I can before I purchase. A particular guitar model may appear to sell for $400, but when you look closely at two of them, that look almost identical, you may find that the model number is one number different or the type of wood used is different, and that could mean one sells for $70 and the other $400. If you pay $200 for it for resale, you will lose money if you get it wrong. Look carefully, take photos, look at items that have SOLD when researching, not items that are listed, because that means nothing. Set your purchase price before you buy. Also be sure to research potential fake or reproduction items. A fake Louis Vuitton (and many other copyrighted brands) will not only cost you big time, it will get you kicked off of eBay instantly and forever.

Research AFTER you buy can also bring in extra profits. I bought a New Orleans area antique document and paid $120, seeing that they typically sold for $300 or so. I decided to use "ancestry" to try to find some of the names listed, and happened upon one of the names on the document as the person who basically developed New Orleans' infrastructure and street layout, which made my $300 document worth $800. Thorough research will earn you additional money both before and after you purchase.

I KNOW NOTHING ABOUT THIS, BUT IT'S SO COOL!

Occasionally, you may see something at a garage sale or estate sale that you think is really "cool" and must be worth a fortune. I found a Civil War era gun powder flask for $50, and bought it, without checking prices. After research, I found that despite the age and war association, it is a fairly common item, and regularly sold for as little as $20 on eBay. I sent it back through a live local auction, and got lucky that someone else thought it was worth much more than it was, too. Don't take chances on an item you know nothing about unless you are willing to lose that money. You may get lucky, but I still make stupid impulse decisions, and impulse buys end badly more often than profitable, even after over 20 years of doing this.

The absolute best thing about research is the knowledge you will acquire and retain. You will never know everything about everything, but the more research you do, the more skills you will acquire in recognizing quality and will eventually be able to identify many items without having to research everything. Possessing this general knowledge will help you buy without spending countless hours trying to figure something out. You will surprise and impress even yourself the first time you see a piece on Antiques Roadshow and can say "that looks like a xxxxx", and then have the expert identify it as exactly what you thought, which brings us to our next chapter. Just be aware that you may become the "go-to" person in your social circle for questions regarding estates/collections, etc., which can be both satisfying and time-consuming.

CHAPTER 6
The "eBay Mentality" and "Antiques Roadshow Syndrome"

There are two different selling formats you can choose on eBay; "Auction" format and "Fixed-Price" format. I am frequently asked about auctioning items on eBay and how to know what price an item will recognize. The reality is that I auction very few items on eBay. My listings are almost exclusively "Buy It Now" (fixed price) listings, mostly because I sell items that I've typically paid more for than I am willing to potentially lose and I don't like the stress of not knowing what I will recognize as an ending price.

Years ago, I would action most everything, but that was in a past era of eBay sales, where few people realized that 99% of items are not nearly as rare as they thought, and before the antiques/collectible market took a huge nose dive because of it. I hate to burst Grandma's bubble about the value of her rare doll collection, but the cold, hard truth is that in almost all cases, you will find a dozen or more of the same dolls listed, and they aren't nearly as rare, nor as valuable as Grandma thinks. That is the definition of ***"The Antiques Roadshow Syndrome"***, as you will learn quickly that the appraisals given on The Antiques Roadshow are typically 5 – 10 times the amount of the eBay value. There are exceptions to this rule, as quality is quality, and quality brings good money, even in times of a bad economy.

The differences in auction vs fixed price listings are huge.

AUCTION FORMAT:

You place an item for sale on eBay for a pre-specified amount of time at a beginning price that you choose as the minimum you will accept. This is a true auction format. People who are looking specifically for your item can find it, and begin to place bids against other people who are looking for that item, as well. Some people start items as low as a $1.00, but be aware of the risk that it may actually sell for that amount and you will lose money.

Pros:

- As long as you set a reasonably low starting price (lower than the actual value), your item WILL sell.

- Cash flow is constant because you will have money at the end of your specified time (1, 3, 5, 7 & 10-day auction formats are available).

- People always seem to want something that other people want. This is the main definition of **"The eBay Mentality"**, and the lower you start your price, the more bids you typically receive, which makes buyers think there is something different or special about your item over the other 15 identical items that are listed....after all, you have 40 bids on yours and the others have only 1 or 2 bids, despite being the exact same item. I have had items sell for almost twice the historical value because of "The EBay Mentality"

- It's exciting. Watching your item receive bids and go up and up in price can be a bit of a rush. Most all auction items will receive the most bidding activity the last 2 minutes of the auction, so try not to get too concerned if the price is not increasing as expected early in the auction.

Cons:

- You are taking a chance that your item may actually sell for less than you paid for it. It's rare, but it has happened to me a few times.
- The item takes much more research to properly describe with good keywords and photograph well to assure you receive top dollar and to make it more attractive than the other identical items listed.
- It can be stressful. EBay offers an option to "watch" an item. Seasoned buyers tend to bid last second. This is called "sniping" an item and can be a rush for a bidder to win at the last second. There are automatic sniping programs available for buyers who use this strategy, so you may get a flurry of bids with as little as 1 or 2 seconds left on the auction. Experienced buyers recognize the eBay Mentality, as well, and know that the more bids an item receives the higher the ending price, so they wait to try to snipe a bargain. Your $40 purchase may have only 8 bids, bringing $20 a half-hour before the auction ends, and will then receive another 20 bids equaling $80 additional within the last 20-30 minutes. You can look at the bid history for past sales and see that trend on most every item with multiple bids. I don't like the stress and I don't like taking chances with my money, so I avoid auctioning anything but lower dollar items unless there is an excellent history of very good ending prices.
- This may be changing, but at this time, you can't require that buyers immediately pay for the item they won, and people sometimes get caught up in bidding on things they regret, or maybe they don't immediately have the money to pay, or maybe they're just a kid, or perhaps they are just an a**hole. You

then end up having to try to chase them down for the money. EBay's system has a non-paying bidder process that is helpful, and eBay will eventually suspend buyers if they repeatedly do not pay for items they win, but it's frustrating and costs you time and a delay in your ability to relist and sell the item.

HINTS FOR SUCCESSFUL AUCTIONING:

As previously mentioned, this is where your research comes in handy. Look at multiple completed listings before you auction something, while eliminating the "buy it now" listings for search parameter results. You want to see that your particular identical item sells over and over again for a certain amount. Find the one that brought the most money and use a similar title and description, because it worked. Do not copy a description verbatim, nor use another seller's photographs. It is considered intellectual property and is against eBay policy to do so. Look at what didn't work with the lowest priced items (bad title, bad feedback for the seller, very short description, etc.) and you will begin to form a good idea of how to list for maximum profit. It's very rare that an item with a good history of consistent ending prices will under-perform. If you're happy with the historical ending price range, then you can feel better about auctioning the item.

If you have an item with no history or one that has multiple items listed, but none are selling, do not auction it. If you start the item at .99 cents, it may sell for that amount if no one is looking for that item. Your time is worth more than that, and it's the best way to assure disappointment.

Don't get stressed out over "zero feedback bidders". Yes, some people have just joined and have no history, but other people use eBay "guest accounts", meaning they don't want eBay to store their payment method online. If someone is repeatedly bidding on your item, and they have a "0" as their feedback rating and just joined eBay the same day they first bid, it can be a red flag, but it can also just be a guest account. Everyone starts with "0" rating, so don't immediately dismiss them.

eBay charges their percentage of the sale to you immediately upon the auction's end, not when the buyer pays, and if you happen to be near the end of your monthly billing cycle, you will have to pay eBay that fee, and will then receive credit in your next billing cycle if a buyer doesn't complete the transaction, so a non-paying bidder can affect your cash flow, as well. You will get all of your fees back, but a buyer has several days to pay once you start a claim, so it can be a long process and you cannot relist the item until the claim is complete.

Describe EVERY flaw and take multiple photos showing those flaws. A buyer can file a "not as described" claim against you and you will end up having to take the item back, pay return shipping and will lose your original cost to ship to the buyer, as well. Shipping is expensive, and it can really hurt on a heavy item where you paid shipping insurance.
Don't let returns frighten you, they are rare. My return rate hovers around 2% and I offer returns for ANY reason. Many sellers do not like offering free returns, but I do on most all of my listings. That then allows you to charge the buyer if the item is damaged and offer a partial refund, and eBay then steps in and pays them the rest. You may also choose to withhold original shipping amount if the buyer returns for any reason other than "not as described" or "damaged". I do not offer free shipping on anything, even though eBay really, really wants sellers to do so, simply because I can state in my listings a sentence of "Free returns accepted for ANY reason, with full item price refunded upon return in same condition". That allows me to withhold the shipping amount the buyer originally paid....otherwise, if you offer free returns and free shipping, you are losing postage both directions out of your pocket, and shipping is sometimes very expensive.

It's just a simple way to assure that the buyer has a little skin in the game, as well, and discourages the scammers (borrowers and thieves…addressed in following chapters) at bay, because they know they will lose the original shipping amount they paid, even if it is a free return for them.

You may have always heard that something's value is equal to what someone is willing to pay for it. With an auction format, something's value is determined in the end by what at least TWO people are willing for pay for it. That's true in both buying and selling via auction.

FIXED PRICE FORMAT:

"Fixed Price" or "Buy It Now" formats for listings, means selling your item for a pre-determined amount, set by you, without the stress of worrying about the ending price.

Fixed price listings are just that….you set the price you want to recognize for the item you are selling. It takes the stress out of the "unknown" ending price when a true auction occurs. You list the item for a fair price; people find the item and hopefully buy it for the price you are asking. On eBay, it's known as a "Buy It Now" listing. Etsy and most other online sales venues don't offer auction format, and almost all of my listings are fixed price listings.

Listing via fixed price makes buying more of a science, as well. As an example, if I find that a particular purse offered at my local auction sells on a regular basis for between $175 – $200 on other "buy it now" ended listings, I know exactly what I can pay for it to maximize my profits. I try my best to make at least a $50 profit on every item I buy, and raise that profit margin, depending on how much money I have to put out to begin with. I will gladly pay $50 or $100 for something I can sell for a $50 profit, but I'm not going to put out $500 on a single item for a $50 profit because that ties up too much cash. Buy it now listings can take days, weeks or even months to sell, so the profit margin I want goes up considerably, based on what I pay at the time of purchase. On a $500 item, I want to make at least a $200 – $300 profit, because it's such a hit to my cash flow. Higher priced items generally take much longer to sell than lower priced ones. Keep that in mind when you are buying. As mentioned before, you make your money when you buy.

The "eBay Mentality" comes into play when pricing your item for sale. Everyone loves a bargain. I know my listings tick off other sellers at times, because if I buy right, I can afford to sell cheaper than every other listing that is currently available for the identical item on eBay. That should be your goal. That purse that I paid $43 for, may show as selling on a regular basis for $175-$200. If I price mine at $165, it will sell quickly. I could price within the same range, but I would then be relying on my good feedback to make buyers choose my item over the others. It certainly helps to have a reputation of quick shipping and happy buyers, I won't diminish that fact, but when it comes down to it, buyers will choose an item where they save $5 and ignore the feedback rating, because in the end, they are protected by eBay if that seller misrepresents the item, anyway. Your goal is to make a profit. If you're greedy, you can slow down your cash flow considerably. I'll take a fast $100 profit over a slow $120 profit any day. The small difference in potential profit isn't worth tying up my cash. If you get greedy and try to recognize maximum profit on every item, you will end up disappointed and frustrated over why your items aren't selling.

Pros of Selling via Fixed Price:

- You know what your profit margin will be. Research carefully; assuring that the item you are researching is the EXACT one you are looking at on ended listings.

If your purse is used, and others have the tag still attached, it isn't going to sell for as much as the new ones. Similarly, it may look identical to one that ended with a good price, but perhaps yours is a less popular color. That will affect price as well. If you research carefully and know what you are buying and what the ending prices are, you're set for a good profit. If yours has the dust bag & box, where others do not, it may be worth a few dollars more. Take all condition variables into consideration when pricing.

- Lack of Stress. The item is listed and you don't have to worry about whether it will recognize a particular price, so you can basically list it and forget about it.

- You have the option of adding a "best offer" option to your listing. Perhaps you list the purse for $165, but knowing you only have $43 into the item, you are actually willing to accept a $150 offer. That's part of the "eBay mentality" of bargain hunting by buyers again. You may get some low ball offers, but if the person is making an offer, then you know they are interested. I may receive an offer of $125, but I know they always sell for at least $175, so I can respond to an offer of $125 with a counter offer of $155, and include a message of

"Thank you for your offer. I am unable to go as low as $125, and as I am sure you have researched, this item typically sells for a minimum of $175, and I am already priced lower than other identical items. However, since you are interested and took the time to contact me, I can offer to you for a quick sale at $155."

Over half of my counter offers are accepted. You made a good profit, the customer feels that they got a bargain, and mutual good feedback and happiness abounds.

- You are able to build up "store" inventory, which prompts buyers to look at your other listings. Buyers love to be able to combine shipping costs if they are interested in more than one of your items. They can also then tag you as a "favorite seller" so they are able to return to your store to check out your new items. I sell such a wide variety of items, that return customers aren't big with me, but if you choose to specialize, it will be huge to you. I also have buyers who let me know in messaging that they are interested in "such and such", which gives me a great list of potential buyers for items I find at auction. I can then contact them after previewing the auction, send photos and ask if they are interested in purchasing if I acquire it. Always, ALWAYS, contact your potential buyer through eBay's messaging system and offer to do a "private listing" for them on eBay if they show interest. If you are caught contacting buyers through eBay to sell things outside of eBay's platform or trying to exchange contact information, you will absolutely have your seller account permanently banned. Listing an item will cost you a few cents per listing per month, based on whether you have a store subscription with eBay or not. Once you have store inventory built up, you can open a subscription "storefront" from eBay for a monthly fee. I have the basic store at $21.95/month. That gives me 1000 free listings per month, so instead of having 350 items renew for 30 cents each, I save money by paying the subscription. There are calculators on eBay that will help you determine if you can save money with a store subscription and will guide you to which type of store is beneficial to you once you build up inventory. My store subscription also provides another benefit of $25 credit every quarter to purchase eBay-branded shipping supplies, so it's $25 in free boxes or tape every 3 months. Not a huge amount, but its $25 in my pocket. It also provides me with free promotional auction style listings if I choose to use them.

Cons of selling via Fixed Price:

- Slower sales/slower cash flow. Your item may take days, weeks or even months to sell. I have had items listed for a year that will suddenly sell. Other times it is purchased within hours of listing. Unlike an auction format, where you know you will have cash flow within 7 days, fixed price sales fluctuate.

- Low-ball offers. Don't take it personally. You will have people who will offer ridiculously low prices for an item you know is worth more. I had a Cartier money clip that was 21.6K solid gold and weighed 12.4 grams. The gold weight alone, if I wanted to sell it to a pawn broker for melt was about $465 at the time. I received offers of $275 on it, although listed for $750 or best offer. I politely declined, explaining the gold melt value and pointing out that the melt value doesn't consider the "Cartier" name associated. I have had them come back, even after that explanation with an offer of $350. Again, I politely declined and depending upon the buyer's attitude, they may get added to my "blocked bidder" list, because at that point, they're just being difficult. People will take a chance and assume that perhaps you don't know what you have and that they can get a bargain of more than they should. You can also set automatic declines under a certain amount within your listing. I don't like doing that, because an offer means the person is interested, and you may be able to make a reasonable sale if you communicate with them.

- Cyclical sales. Christmas is a great time to be a seller. Even early January, when people are using their cash gifts to buy is good. February stinks. I have had sales of over $12,000 in December, to have that drop to $500 in February. Save your money for those slim times. When taxes are due, it's slow....when tax refunds begin to be received in March & April, it's good. Mother's Day has a bit of a rush on gift items for Mom...August is horrible, because people have spent their money on vacations and/or are buying school clothes/items for their kids. I try to make a minimum of $700 weekly in profits ($1400 or so in sales) because that's what I need to pay my bills. $1000 profit weekly is nice ($2000 in sales), and anything over that profit amount is business cash flow, which is either used to purchase more inventory and/or squirreled away for hard times, which hit in February and August for me. Depending on what you sell, you will recognize those hard times are approaching and target your purchases towards things that may be needed. I don't typically sell shoes, but found a huge lot of Brand New Ed Hardy Tennis Shoes in the Box at auction and bought 30 pairs. Despite August being slow, those shoes sold because they were great as a back to school item. Carefully plan and target both your purchases and sales around those slow times, as well as your economic needs. I tend to buy faster than I can list, so I typically have an inventory of unlisted items to sell during slow times when I need all of the money I make, or I will paint a couple of pieces of furniture and find other items to sell on local markeplaces during that time to supplement income.

As previously mentioned, despite whether you choose auction format or fixed price format for your listings, your research and fair pricing will be the two most important aspects for success.

CHAPTER 7
Beg, Borrow and Steal (Nightmare Buyers)

You may have heard the stories about buyers on eBay and how sellers are at a disadvantage when it comes to dealing with the difficult ones. Just as in real life, the nightmare customers are few and far between, but we tend to only hear stories about the bad ones....why even mention a sale that went well? That's not interesting...we want to hear the drama...but you don't want to deal with it while selling on eBay. We all know people who are not capable of common sense, those who are impossible to satisfy no matter how hard you try, and of course, the worst kind....those who will try to get something for free, either because they are cheap or just because they are a person without conscience and no better than a common thief. I have run into at least one of each on eBay, and thankfully, they are the minority. Just as 99% of sellers are good, decent and honest people, 99% of buyers are the same. That doesn't make having to deal with the 1% any easier. eBay & most marketplaces are weighted heavily towards protection of the Buyer, but most do have Seller protection policies as well. Familiarize yourself with those protection policies, and then read what I've experienced as supplemental, because they will not teach you about the Beggars and Borrowers, and they do not want you to even know about the Thieves.

As I've said before, you will never be at a high enough level of "smart" to overcome some people's level of "dumb". Those people are the least painful to deal with....at least they are typically good people, who are just not too bright (bless their hearts). I'm pretty good at "stupid-proofing" my listings and spelling out terms & conditions that would preempt most problems. Even with that, you can never plan for those who have graduated with their Masters in "stupid" until they beat you with it, and the attacks come unexpectedly and with a new lesson every time. For items such as the collectible perfume bottle that I previously discussed, where the 50 year old perfume inside was no longer fresh, I now include "item sold for collectible value and contents may be expired" on perfumes or liquid of any type. Lesson learned, and I am positive that I will continue to learn difficult lessons from these buyers. I can't even address how to protect yourself against this buyer, because, like I said, you just can't plan for a surprise attack of stupidity. Those buyers are the least of your worries. The ones to watch out for are those looking to beg, borrow and steal. I will cover some methods you can use to best protect your business against them.

THE BEGGAR

This is the buyer who gets an item, finds even the tiniest issue that you didn't mention, and then begs for a discount instead of returning it. They may have also spent more than they could afford and/or purchased on impulse, sometimes even when drinking. They also tend to be the ones who try unsuccessfully to get a bargain before the sale, and just aren't happy unless they can get a few dollars back from you after the sale. You may even get messages with sob stories from them. The "Beggars" know that eBay is buyer friendly, and if they can find anything wrong, they know they have you over a barrel due to eBay's buyer-friendly protection. They are still thieves, but at least you can fight them easily.

THE BORROWER

Gucci Earrings – check; Size 10 Black Cocktail Dress – check; Jimmy Choo Shoes – check.

This is the buyer who only wants your item temporarily to fill their need, after which they plan to return to you for a full refund. Jewelry, clothing & other accessories are the main targets for the Borrower. They are also still thieves, stealing your time, your ability to actually sell the item, and any postage costs you have to cover.

THE THIEF

Just as in a storefront business, these people are the lowest of the low. They want the item, especially a high-end item, but they don't want to pay for it, or perhaps they have a damaged identical item and want a replacement that is not damaged, or your real Louis Vuitton is almost identical to their fake one. They can't walk into your home or business to take it as a conventional thief would, and you are hundreds or thousands of miles away from them, so you present very little threat of retribution. These buyers will ask for a return and send you an empty box, their old damaged item or the fake and may even remove parts for electronics repairs. They may even send a completely different item that weighs the same, but isn't what you sold to them. One reseller I know received a box of trash. These folks are the rarest of scammers on eBay, but they do exist. They don't care if others are harmed with their actions. They are scum.

Let's start by covering the "Beggar".

Scenario #1: I want a freebie/discount. You sell a $10 item with $5 postage. The buyer has paid $15. They receive the item and look it over with a fine tooth comb and find a tiny scratch on the bottom left corner. They message you and complain. Your item is now "not as described" if you did not mention that tiny scratch and eBay will force you to accept a return AND pay for return shipping of $5.00. You now have to refund the buyer $15 and pay another $5.00 to have it returned. That $10 sale just cost you $10 additional dollars. The buyer knows you are not going to sink another $5.00 into a return, and that many sellers will just choose to tell them to keep it and then refund the $15 to avoid losing another $5 on an item that isn't worth your time to relist. They want the item, they just want it cheaper, and most likely, they really have no intention of returning it (although you can't tell if they do or not).

Scenario #2: I overspent. A buyer purchases and pays for an item. They get it, and then realize that they overspent, or stupidly went on a drunken shopping spree (some of my best sales are between midnight and 5 am on Friday & Sat nights). Occasionally, they will contact you prior to shipping and ask you to cancel the sale. Just cancel it and then grumble to yourself quietly. EBay offers a "cancellation" option where you can send a cancellation that says "buyer changed mind". You refund, they accept the cancellation and you get your fees back, and then you add them to your blocked bidder list. You then have to relist the item and start over with it, and now other buyers may now think there is something wrong with the item because it sold before and here it is again! I normally add a statement at the beginning of the description of "due to a non-paying bidder, this item is being re-listed". That takes the question in other buyers' minds away. That person is the easy one to deal with. The one that is a pain is that the person actually lets you ship, then they make up a reason for return. I discourage overspending buyers by charging shipping on my listings. If you offer free shipping, then the refund to the buyer is 100% of what they paid. If you charge shipping separately, and you offer free returns, you can at least withhold the original shipping the buyer paid. It can be a double-edge sword, though. The buyer may know that they you can withhold original shipping they paid, and if they are savvy, they will claim not as described" as their reason for return, though most are not that savvy. You can also report a buyer to eBay (and should) for dishonest behavior. You also have the opportunity to withhold up to 50% of the item's original price if they return it damaged.

Scenario #3: The straight up Beggar. A buyer receives an item, tells you honestly that they overspent, or perhaps they claim an emergency has come up and they need the money back and would like to return the item. I accept returns for any reason, mostly because it keeps a buyer from purposely damaging an item in order to be able to return it. Most people are honest. If someone seems honest and just says that they overspent, I will normally accept the return, tell them that original shipping amount will be withheld, then refund the purchase price of the item only. If you offer free shipping, then you must refund 100% to meet eBay policy.

Protection against these scenarios:

1. Add postal insurance to everything unless you are willing to lose it. You can file a claim if the buyer says something is damaged, and then gently remind them

that you need detailed photos to go along with their written statement of damage You can casually say *"so sorry for the inconvenience, but postal services are investigating more and more felony insurance fraud claims and your statement and photos will help expedite my claim"*. If they're lying, they typically go away with the thought of an investigation and potential charges.

2. Within your listing, describe every imperfection you see, as well as photos of that imperfection. Look closely at your items prior to listing and take/save multiple photos (in addition to those you use within your listing).

3. A statement within your description of "this item is pre-owned and may show very light signs of wear, such as light overall scratching, as expected". This simple statement will protect you against petty complaints. An honest person, if they are concerned, will ask in advance for photos or a better description of those scratches & scuffs because they fully intend on keeping the item.

4. Another favorite complaint of the beggar is "odor"...it's unprovable, it's subjective and is an easy thing for a buyer to choose as a complaint...after all, you can't dispute or photograph an odor like you can if they claim a scratch that isn't really there. They may sometimes say that they are going to have to have the piece professionally laundered and will cost them $xx, which they want back from you. Just add a statement in your listing of fabric items that says "items are obtained from a variety of sources, and I do not have the history of the prior owner's habits or storage method. Item may contain residual odors such as perfumes, moth balls, smoke, etc. If you are sensitive to odors, please consider this prior to purchase." That will eliminate returns at your cost due to the "odor" complaint. I have not fully regained

my sense of smell after contracting Covid, so I include this on every fabric listing.

5. Never take immediate responsibility for a reported issue. Always ask the buyer questions until you feel comfortable that the problem is your fault. My favorite was a pre-owned Cartier bracelet where the buyer said "I'm going to have to return this ($300) bracelet, it keeps coming unhooked and falling off my wrist". I had worn the bracelet a few nights prior myself and had no issues with it at all, so I knew this was a made-up reason, either due to regret or she wanted a discount or was a Borrower, and wanted me to have to pay postage. I messaged her back and said, *"thanks for letting me know. I wore the bracelet a few days ago and didn't have an issue, but my wrist is large enough to keep a bracelet of this size from losing tension. Has the hook closure become damaged, and if so, could you send a photo, or is it because of the size of your wrist?"*. She replied that it was because her wrist was small and the tension hook closure allowed it to open. Bingo....it's a size problem, not a problem with the item, and I had listed the exact size of the piece, so I then politely informed her that I accept returns for any reason, but original postage costs will be withheld and since the security tag was no longer attached, a partial refund would be issued, as my listings state that "full refunds issued for return in same condition with security tag intact". It would have been up to a $160 loss for her, so she kept the bracelet. Remember, if you offer free returns, you can withhold 50% of the item price upon return if not in same condition.

6. Take more photos than you use in the listing. I typically take 20 photos to get the 10-12 photos I used in the listing, but I keep all 20. An arsenal of additional photos of every item you sell WILL come to your rescue against the Beggar, and these photos should be kept for at least 180 days after a sale

(Credit Card/PayPal's limit on claims). You may not have put a close-up photo of the bottom left corner on the eBay listing, and the buyer claims a scratch, but you are then able to respond with, *"Hi buyer. Attached to this message is a photo of the bottom left corner in question and I do not show a scratch. Could you please forward a photo of the damage, so that I can have proof for a postal insurance claim?"* All of this correspondence is done within eBay's communication system, and when a liar is caught, you will most likely not hear from them again. The risk with this protection method is that they may now actually damage the item to the extent they claimed, but their goal is a discount, so that is rare. You will then have to accept the return or fight it with eBay as the mediator if you can't make them back down. This is another reason for the photos and insurance. You can also send those photos to eBay if the buyer opens a claim and you have a much better chance of winning that claim if you can prove condition, or show that you mentioned that minor scratches may exist. Your preparation before listing will assure more wins than losses. Just a note that eBay counts cases against you as a seller if you ask them to step in and then lose the case, so choose your battles wisely to keep your seller rating high. I would only fight higher dollar cases. You are allowed only a 2% "defect" rating, which includes late shipments, lost cases and seller cancelled transactions if you break or lose an item before shipment. Below that rating is "below standard" and if it gets too bad, your fees go up and you could lose the right to sell.

7. Take a chance that the buyer doesn't know how far they can push with eBay. Most of the Beggars will not open a case/claim through eBay's system because they want a discount on an item they actually wanted and they really don't want to return it. They exhibit that behavior on every item they buy, so they do not

want eBay involved, because that behavior is against eBay policies. I make it a personal policy to just answer their message and say, "No problem on the return. Please open a return case and send back at your earliest convenience." If they open a case/claim, you may end up having to refund everything, but the buyer most likely wants the item and you don't hear back from them in many cases or they never ship the item if they have opened a case....they were just taking a shot at a discount, where repeated behavior like this isn't registered against them through eBay's system. If they do not ship back to you within 5 business days of a return case being opened and accepted by you, you can call eBay on Day #6 and have the case closed in your favor, and the buyer no longer has the option of a return, and any negative feedback they may leave can be removed.

8. Build a couple of extra dollars into the price of every item to cover these claims. You may just choose to offer a small discount. I normally do not choose this option, because I feel it only encourages bad buyer behavior and because my seller rating can handle a couple of problems without penalty, but it will most likely assure good feedback, a good customer service history with eBay and if you have it covered by an extra dollar or two in the price of every item, it really doesn't cost you anything. It's an option for new sellers, especially, where you can't really afford negative feedback or problems that could affect your future ability to sell. A discount is what they wanted, they get it. You block them from ever bidding on your items again in eBay's "blocked bidder list", and you can then report them to eBay for abusing the buyer protection program. The buyer doesn't know you have reported them, and if they are doing this to multiple sellers who are reporting them, that buyer will have their eBay account eventually suspended.

9. Many sellers disagree with me on this point, but I say that you should never leave feedback as a seller until the buyer leaves feedback for you. Savvy buyers know that they can hold you as a "feedback hostage". Negative feedback can be removed if it was threatened and used as a negotiating tool by a buyer, but it has to be clear extortion, such as "if you don't give me $5.00 back on this, I'll leave bad feedback". In the same manner that buyer's know they hold you as a hostage, because you have not yet left feedback, they know that you also have some leverage. Believe it or not, eBay does not allow a seller to leave negative or neutral feedback for a buyer. It's positive feedback or nothing, but many buyers do not realize this. You can respond to bad feedback if someone leaves you a negative, but you cannot give them the same negative record that they can give to you. You can, however, leave positive feedback on THEIR page and then say, "Offered multiple resolution options including refund", or "Thanks for returning the item so quickly". As a seller, I regularly check the feedback of the person who has purchased an item, and also check the feedback they have left for other sellers. If they are a repeat offender, a few "positive-negative" comments will begin to affect them. EBay doesn't like it, but as long as you do not personally attack the person, and state only truthful facts while sounding nice, you can do it. You can't call them "difficult" (or any other names) on feedback. I regularly block potential buyers who ask suspicious sounding questions if their feedback indicates this type of behavior.

Many of these protection methods will apply to Borrowers and Thieves, as well. Your most important protection is your inspection and preparation. It will become second nature and will take very little time to protect yourself once you set up a template of the general language within your terms & conditions that will address 90% of the methods that the Beggars, Borrowers and Thieves use. Your terms & conditions will be the "fine print" in your listing that honest people will ignore, but those looking to take advantage will review carefully and move on to an easier target.

Again, I would like to stress that these buyers are the rare exception, not the rule, but if you can save yourself the headache of having to deal with them in the first place, that's the best scenario.

THE BORROWER

To recap, the "Borrower" is the buyer who has a temporary need for your item, and really has no intention of keeping it, and will return it after they "borrow" it. Anything that can be used and returned without signs of use can be targets for the Borrower, but in my experience, jewelry & clothing are the two main targets.

I had multiple pieces of very high end jewelry "borrowed" over the years, and the most likely time for that to occur is just before Christmas. Office parties, weddings, special events, etc., creates a need for people to buy a special outfit or good jewelry. After all, you don't really have much need for a diamond cocktail cluster ring on a regular basis, but it's nice to have one when you dress up. So why don't we all have multiple pieces of really good jewelry to choose from? Because it's expensive, of course! This is especially true during the Christmas season, when you're buying gifts for everyone and running up debt on credit cards. Most all of us are on a budget and a $500 Tiffany necklace purchase just isn't part of the normal plan...but it sure would look good at that party to impress the co-workers.

I'll touch on the return policies, but those are readily available within the selling site you use in much more detail.

- To be eligible for top rated status, which earns you a 10% discount on your eBay fees, you must accept returns for up to 30 days. In December, when I have sold as much as $10,000-$12,000, that 10% discount on my 12-13% fees can mean an appx $160 savings for the month, so it can be a decent savings that you will want to be able to recognize.
- If the item is "not as described", buyers can request a return up to 45 days after purchase through eBay and you may have to honor that return if eBay finds in favor of the buyer. Credit Card Companies/PayPal is even worse. Not only do you have to worry about eBay's return policies, they a 180-day return policy, where the buyer can dispute the transaction. ***As a side note of protection, print screen shots of delivery confirmation and keep them in a folder on your computer by the week or month. The postal carriers typically only keep delivery confirmation information available for 120 days. The thieves know this and will open a case between the 120 & 180 day period, claiming they did not receive or did not authorize the purchase. They know that you most likely cannot provide delivery confirmation without significant effort on your part to try to get the Post office to search their archives.*** Keep all of your eBay emails for reference, because your sold items are purged from eBay, along with tracking info about every 90 days and your only access to tracking numbers will be that email. If a chargeback is filed through a credit card/PayPal, that will trigger eBay to place a hold on your funds, and depending upon payment options you have provided, they may even have access to your bank account to be able to draft the funds, whether you agree with them or not. Always set up a separate bank account to associate with your eBay account. I have a business account, where I keep a minimal amount of money, so that nothing can affect

my ability to pay my mortgage or power bill. That buys me some time to deal with eBay being owed if it comes to that.

- You can opt out of returns for eBay, but if a customer gets something and they claim it's "not as described", you will need an excellent argument to be able to keep from having to take that return, and will then be responsible to pay for return shipping, as well as losing your original shipping cost. If a Credit Card/PayPal chargeback is filed, they couldn't care less if you choose to accept returns or not. They will follow their rules, despite your rules or eBay's rules.

- Not accepting returns has been shown to increase the chances of a buyer lying about the reason for return. They may break the item, damage it, or just say something is wrong in order to force a return, where if you easily accept returns, you can at least get your item back in good enough condition to resell. You will have to weigh the options and decide for yourself how to wish to handle your own return policy.

-

Doesn't sound fair, huh? Well, sellers are currently awaiting the outcome of ongoing lawsuits because eBay is really just 3rd party money handlers and sellers are not their employees. They are bound to be an unbiased middle man to protect both buyers & sellers, but they overwhelmingly side with the buyer, so hopefully the lawsuits will change that, and in the meantime, it's somewhat better than it used to be. For now, though, it's just the way it is, and like I said, it's a rare occurrence, so it's not a huge deal for most sellers. It's a part of doing business, and at least you can write off losses on your taxes. My personal return rate is about 2%, and I accept returns for any reason, so it's typically a very small amount of your overall sales.

Back to the Borrowers. Most borrowers probably don't really think that they are causing harm to anyone. They tend to think "I'll just buy this, and return it and get my money back, and the seller can resell it...no harm, no foul, right?" Wrong! It doesn't seem bad on the surface, but these are the ways the Borrower harms you:

1. Cash Flow. You think you've made a $500 sale, and after all, it's Christmas or back to school time, or your mortgage is due, so you spend the money. Suddenly, 3 weeks later, you get a return request. Now you're getting the item back, and you will owe the buyer $500 when you get it. It hurts unless you have a huge reserve of cash. The return can also hit when you are close to your monthly fees payment to eBay, and you will have to pay them their commission of $50 on that item, and then get a credit on your next statement if the return crosses over the due date for fee payments.

2. Your Item is now devalued. I have found that Borrowers are also Beggars. They overwhelmingly want a discount on the item because they don't want a large amount of their money held up while they borrow the item. Every sale shows on eBay's "sold" page and the history for the item you sold to them at a discount stays there, even if the item is returned. Now you get back an item that shows you took a discount once before so it is now devalued because everyone will want the discount. New potential buyers can also easily figure out that the item was returned, so they automatically think something is wrong with it, so it's more difficult to sell.

3. Inability to sell the item quickly. Once the buyer decides to return, they have 5 business days to actually show that they have shipped the item. The item can then take another 5 business days to get to you. They've had the item for 3 weeks, so now you have an item that has been gone for over a month. Christmas is over and your chance of selling a good item during the most opportune time to sell is gone.

4. Loss of money. Even if the buyer is honest and just returns because they don't like it, you lose any return shipping costs, insurance, signature confirmation and packaging supplies, plus your time. They are still stealing from you.

5. A Borrower lies or damages/ruins your item. Some borrowers, who don't care that they are harming you and feel they are entitled somehow, may claim something is wrong with the item, or even worse, may damage it after they use it in order to get you to pay return shipping. A $500 small item can easily cost you $20 in postage, insurance and signature confirmation....both ways. That's a $40 loss. If they have damaged the item, I lose what I paid for it, as well. It can add up, especially on expensive items. Unfortunately, it's a part of doing business and your comfort will be in taking the tax write-off at the end of the year. You may be able to recoup this through a postal insurance claim, but you can't count on it.

6. Damage to your Seller Account. If you choose to fight the return and lose the case, it's counted as a "defect" against your seller account. Too many strikes can cause eBay to place limits on the volume of your sales, suspend you for a time, or suspend you permanently. You have to perform as a fair seller in order to be able to sell in what is presented as a safe marketplace for buyers. It just isn't worth fighting in the long run unless you have indisputable proof, which is difficult to do. In most cases, it is just better to write it off on your taxes and move on.

Ways to help protect yourself against the Borrower:

The best way to protect yourself against the Borrower is to be proactive PRIOR to a potential sale. Once a buyer has the item in hand, eBay's policies will protect them if they decide to take advantage, so you want to deter and discourage them from choosing your items in the first place.

1. **Blocking**: EBay allows you to block certain bidders from purchasing your items within their pre-set parameters. I can choose to block buyers who have had a certain number of non-paying bidder reports, who have been reported by other sellers for abusing return or other eBay policies, or I can individually block buyers if I am not comfortable selling to them. You may get a bad feeling about someone who is begging for a discount, or who gets angry because you won't accept their low-ball offer, or maybe you can tell that they are just plain nuts. You can read the feedback they left for other sellers and if don't like what you see, or maybe other sellers have left feedback, even though it must be positive, that says "Buyer returned item in good condition", you can choose to block them. That's a seller signal to other sellers that this buyer is a Borrower. I look at that information every time I receive an offer. You can choose to block them easily with a "block bidder" function that eBay provides for your account.

2. **A clear return policy**. EBay's policies will override your policies, period. Borrowers aren't typically purposeful thieves, so if they intend to borrow your item, they may actually pay attention to your return policy. Remember, they are looking for an easy target with no drama for the return, and if your policies are strong, they may decide to move on. Your policies may or may not hold water with eBay if push comes to shove, but most borrowers won't know that unless they are a professional eBay thief. I have things such as this within my terms & conditions on every listing:

    - *"I offer 30-day returns for any reason in my listings, Full item price refund issued upon return in same condition with all inclusions"*. (They now know they lose shipping costs.)

- *"I pay full insurance and signature confirmation on every item over $100 in value. Returns must be sent via same shipping method originally used and must include full value insurance and signature confirmation in order to qualify for full refund".* (The borrower now realizes that return shipping is going to be $20, not $3, and they look at that as a cost of rental that they didn't want to have to pay. Ebay will not stand by this policy, but the buyer typically doesn't know that and the borrower moves on to another listing Honest people will pay no attention to this.)

3. **Security Section** – what I feel is the most important deterrent to Borrowers. My security section reads, *"item will arrive with a tamper-proof holographic "void if removed", individually numbered security tag attached. RETURNS MUST HAVE tag intact to qualify for full refund."*

   I purchased 100 of these individually numbered stickers for $9.99 off of eBay and wrap them through jewelry openings. They stick to themselves or to the item and can't be removed and put back on if tightly secured, because they will peel and show "void" on the back. No one is going to wear a piece of jewelry with this tag hanging off of it. It also works through button holes or zipper pulls on clothing items and over screws of electronics so they can't be opened and parts removed, and at a cost of 9 cents per item, it's more than worth it. I obviously do not use these on every item, as no one is going to borrow an antique vase, but on jewelry, high end purses/clothing/shoes, etc., electronics or other high risk items, they are a must.

Again, eBay will not stand by this warning, but the goal is to deter the borrowers or thieves BEFORE they buy. They see this and move on to a different victim.

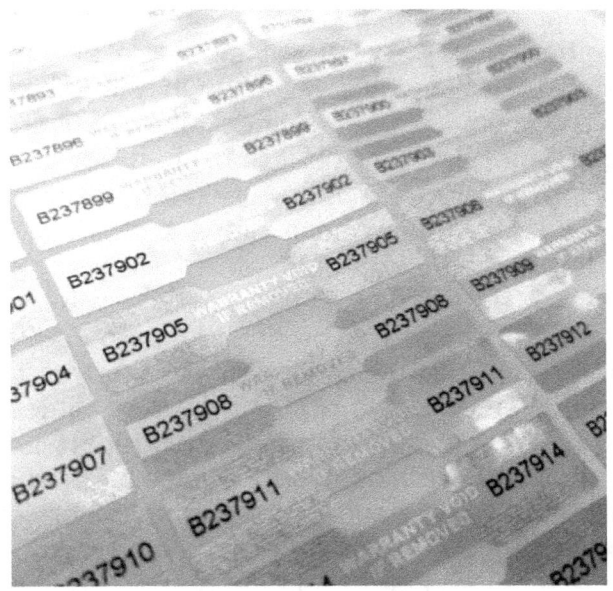

After the Sale Protection:

1. If a return case is opened because the buyer says something is wrong, request photos before accepting the return. You have already told them that you have multiple photos, and they have no idea what the photos show that they didn't see within the listing. This will sometimes make the return request go away. If not, you may actually have a photo you took that shows that what they already claimed is incorrect, and now the item is not in the same condition as received and is not eligible for a return or is at least eligible for a postal insurance claim. As an example, I

had a buyer who purchased a watch and then claimed it was a woman's watch, not a man's. I had not uploaded a photo of the model # that was shown on the back of the watch to the listing, but I had a photo of it, which matched the manufacturer website serial number for a man's watch. He then had to choose whether to pay return shipping himself or keep the watch. He kept the watch. On the other hand, a buyer claimed that a necklace pendant had a significant dark spot on it that I had not disclosed. I had not noticed it, but sure enough, there it was in a photo I had taken, so it helps the buyer, and your customer service reputation when you've made a mistake, as well. You can bet you will make those errors on occasion. You can't force the buyer to send photos. EBay doesn't require a buyer to provide them in order to file a claim, so sometimes you just have to accept the return and then report the buyer to eBay. You can also use eBay's seller protection (you have to call eBay and fight for it), to cover your losses if you find the buyer lied about damage that is not there when you get the item back. Those losses are typically given as a credit on your seller statement. Choose carefully if you decide to demand seller protection. EBay does not often cover it, and if you've used it a couple of times, they will begin to blame you for the problems, not their own system, and will reject your request. Save it for infrequent, larger dollar losses.

2. When a return case is open, mention in the acceptance that signature confirmation is required for a return on high dollar items. They may not do it, but if they do, that provides you the opportunity to open it in front of a postal employee/postman as a witness in case you receive a different item than expected. Postal fraud is a federal felony level offense. You may also choose to report to the IC3 report, which is the Internet Crime Complaint Center, who

investigates theft/fraud for internet transactions. Report the buyer to eBay immediately and use postal employee's contact info in your correspondence with eBay as proof, offering their written statement, and a copy of the postal/IC3 claim you have opened as backup documentation. This is more of a protection measure against the "Thief", not the "Borrower", but you don't really know yet which one the buyer may be. You can also file an actual police report for theft, although those investigations typically go nowhere.

3. Report the buyer if they misused the return policy. If the buyer claimed something is wrong and it isn't, report them to eBay. It most likely won't help you in your immediate situation, but that report may be the final strike it takes to suspend them from eBay if other sellers have also reported them for the same thing. It will eventually catch up to them if sellers report abuse as they should, and ebay may even give you a credit.

4. Block the buyer from ever bidding on another one of your items. EBay provides you with a tool in their system to have a "blocked bidders" list. There are websites dedicated to scam buyer IDs and you can block from those pages, but really, what are the chances, out of tens of millions of buyers that you will come across that particular scammer? I see those sites as a waste of time unless you sell one particular item, such as Apple Products and there is a known scammer for those particular items. Buyers sometimes have multiple accounts and could potentially buy from you again. If you feel this has happened, check contact info for the past problem and see if any of it matches, cancel the transaction, and report them to eBay on that account, as well.

5. IF the buyer leaves you good feedback, then go to their feedback and leave a positive feedback comment (remember, you can't leave negative or neutral for a buyer), and leave a seller "code" comment such as, "Sorry the item didn't work out.

Thanks for returning quickly", that other sellers may see. If they leave you bad or neutral feedback, leave something stronger, such as "accepted return, provided full refund, left neg :'(", which will also let other sellers know they are a difficult buyer. On your own feedback, you can be a bit harsher than that, by responding "impossible buyer can't be satisfied. Returned, rec'd full refund. Avoid". If the buyer has not left feedback for you, don't leave it for them. It is important that you not respond to their feedback comment before contacting eBay. If you accept free returns, a buyer cannot leave negative feedback (one of the perks of free returns), and eBay will remove their comment. However, if you have responded, they will not remove it.

Now for the worst of the bunch….the Thieves.

This is the person who enters a transaction with the forethought of stealing your item and then sees an opportunity because of lack of protection on your side, to do so.

Your preparation to prevent a thief from wanting to target you is your best protection, but even then, if they are determined, you will most likely lose an item….and money. I like to think of the preventative measures as a locked door & windows on your home. It really isn't going to stop a thief, but an unlocked door & windows lets them in easily with no deterrent and may actually provide an opportunity they wouldn't have taken, had you simply locked the door. Even if you have the best security system in the world, a determined thief can be smart and evil, and you need to be one step ahead. Nothing is going to guarantee that they won't be able to steal, but there are measures you can take, both before and after a sale to make it more difficult for them.

I cannot stress enough that you should never accuse or treat someone like they are a thief. There are honest mistakes that may make you think they are a thief...such as a child bringing a package inside and not telling their parents. A neighbor saw the package and picked it up, thinking they were doing a favor to keep it from being stolen and just hasn't taken it to them yet, or a postman left it at the wrong address or placed in the wrong box. Always ask that the buyer check with family members and neighbors in case of a mis-delivery or in case someone picked it up that they are unaware of. Even if you think they are a thief, EBay does not like accusatory or foul language, so always be professional and cautiously take the buyer at their word and assume they are telling the truth....until it's obvious they are not. Then handle it through eBay, not through the thief.

Ways that online thieves can steal from you

1. Claims item was never received.

2. Says that box was received empty.

3. Requests return, sends back an empty box, or a box with a rock.

4. Claims item was not as described, and returns an identical used item they own, or a fake item that is similar.

5. Talks you into shipping to an "unconfirmed" address by saying they will be away, or it's a "gift" for someone. EBay/PayPal only protects you if you ship to a confirmed address. DO NOT change one letter of the address provided by eBay and assure that it states "eligible for seller protection" beside the buyer's address. If it doesn't, cancel the transaction and make them correct the address and repurchase the item prior to shipping.

6. It is impossible to cover every scenario of how to respond to the thieves once they have your item. I try my best to prevent the theft prior to the sale. Check the buyer's feedback, especially the "feedback left for others" before you complete a sale. It's better to cancel if you aren't comfortable than to lose an expensive item.

    Cancelling sales too often will result in "strikes" against your seller account, but there is a trick to cancelling and making it the buyer's decision. Message the buyer and tell them that you dropped and broke the item (or that you ripped it, spilled coffee on it, etc.), and ask if they still want it. As soon as they say "no", you can cancel the transaction for reason of "buyer requested cancellation", which is not a strike and has no impact on your seller account. You can also cancel for reason of "problem with buyer's address" with no penalty. I tease that if I'm ever asked by eBay as to what the problem is with the address (and I've never been asked), that I am going to respond with "A scammer lives there." This is a bit of a gray area as far as honesty goes, but I'm the only one who can protect my business and eBay offers no help to sellers when the hairs on the back of your neck stand up. You can make your own decision as to whether this is too deep of a shade of gray for you. No judgment.

7. Many sellers don't like long sections of "terms & conditions" in their listings. I find that the language I use that was mentioned above has protected me on more than one occasion and are fairly short statements that can be formatted in smaller text at the end of the description. I am not claiming that this language will protect you after the sale when it comes down to a case and if the thief if really intent on having your item. EBay is still very buyer friendly, and terms in your listing may or may not be upheld by

eBay, so you may still lose your item. However, the purpose is to make honest buyers feel good about your protection measures and accommodations for them, while making it unattractive to thieves, who want easy money and an easy target. If a buyer claims through PayPal instead of eBay, just accept the return unless you have extremely clear proof. If you lose a case through PayPal, they will not require the item to be returned to you, so you are out the item and the money.

8. The next chapter will get a little deeper into the "customer service" verbiage. It will also contain some language that will protect after a sale. Undoubtedly, you WILL have a buyer who is not happy, who can be confrontational, or may outright accuse you of trying to rip them off. Handling those people with grace and professionalism becomes difficult at times, but after working construction for 30 years, a field where you have to protect yourself in every bit of correspondence sent because of potential consequences, I have learned how to handle angry people, without acquiescing to their every whim...all while still protecting myself....and while making them feel good about it.

CHAPTER 8
The Art of Diplomacy
(aka, "Being Able to Tell Someone to Go to Hell and Making Them Look Forward to the Trip")

A very important part of being an eBay Seller is your communication with your buyer. It's important enough that eBay includes it as a "Star Rating" category on how well you communicate as part of the evaluation of your right to sell using their platform. A low communication rating can affect your ability to sell as much as not shipping on time, or having multiple "not as described" reports. Most transactions require very little communication. You get questions, you answer them. You get a notification that something has sold, and the buyer automatically receives notification that the item has shipped. You receive feedback and you provide feedback. However, every now and then, you will encounter an overly bothersome or outright annoying, difficult, crazy, or lying buyer. That's where your skill within the art of diplomacy in communications will work to your benefit.

Every bit of communication you and the Buyer sends through eBay's system is viewable by eBay personnel, and is strongly weighted when it comes to disputes. You will always want to make sure that all of your communication is extremely professional and completed through eBay's system. If you receive an email or even a phone call from a buyer (eBay gives buyers your contact info after a sale), message them through eBay, copy & paste their email and ask them to communicate only through eBay, so that you are both following eBay policy. I cannot stress strongly enough that even if you know, beyond a shadow of a doubt that the buyer is lying, you are to never indicate or accuse them of that within written communication to them. Always, always, talk to the Buyer as if they are completely innocent. Respect, even if undeserved, will go a long way in making your buyer easier to handle, will put you in a better position with eBay if a case escalates, and will calm a situation immensely. It also makes a real scammer more comfortable because they think that you do not recognize their scam, which puts you in a position of power.

I have received messages from buyers who have outright called me a cheat or a liar, yet I have only one bad feedback in over 20 years. A buyer was obviously buying real designer items and then returning fakes to sellers. Her feedback to other sellers indicated multiple returns. She had a total feedback rating of 9 transactions. 5 of her feedback comments to other sellers said things like "great seller, had an issue, handled professionally", and "seller accepted return without question-will buy from again".
These are comments that should raise your suspicion. I had a Dior purse with a receipt from the store where it was purchased, but did not offer the receipt with the listing because it had other items included that had been purchased at the same time, and I had sold the bag for more than I had paid off of a clearance rack, which can irritate a buyer. Always remove or black out the price of an item if it's less than what a buyer paid. The buyer received the bag, claimed it was dirty and in horrible condition, a fake, and wanted to return it. It was brand new, with tags, never used. I knew immediately it was a scam and sent a picture of the receipt. Her return was refused, she threw a hissy fit, and she left bad feedback. I reported her to eBay and pointed out her feedback and return history and she ended up being kicked off of eBay within 24 hours. Back then, eBay did not remove feedback, but I was able to leave negative feedback for her before she was suspended, as, "scam artist who buys authentic and tries to return fakes. Beware", which warned other sellers who may be experiencing the same thing with her (oh, how I long for those days of eBay).

Looking back, had I handled the communication better, I would not have responded to her, would have contacted eBay with the receipt and had her kicked off before she had the opportunity to leave that feedback. I was still an inexperienced seller. I want you to be better prepared than I was.

Over the past 30 years, I have learned more in my Construction background about communication skills than I thought I would ever need to know. Construction is an industry where saying the wrong thing can cost you tens of thousands of dollars. I honed my skills of being able to empathize with people, while still protecting myself and making them feel good about it. I can offer a couple of examples here of verbiage to use, but obviously cannot address every scenario. Hopefully, this will help you begin to look at things in a way that not only communicates that you believe the buyer, but that you also empathize with them and are trying to help, all while still protecting yourself as a first priority.

Knowing eBay's policies inside and out when it comes to returns will be your best ammunition. Just as I had to know my subcontractor's jobs and contract terms better than they did, I have to know eBay policies better than their call center employees. You will find over time, that the level of knowledge and answers you get from eBay customer service representatives will vary greatly and are mostly read from a notebook. If you get a foreign representative on the phone, pretend you have a bad connection and call back. The low-level customer service representatives at eBay cannot make decisions, give horrible advice and are of more harm than help in many cases. Very few buyers know the rules as well as you, and I make it my job to know the rules better than most of eBay's own employees. I can point them to their own rules if necessary. By being able to quote eBay's policies, you take yourself out of the equation as the villain.
(I used to use my liability insurance company and the

lending bank on a project as the villain in my Construction business). Once people think something is out of your control, it's more difficult for them to be disagreeable with you. Just as a waitress is not responsible for the quality of the food you are served (and I hope you would never choose to punish a waitress for something the cook did), you are not responsible for writing the policies that you and the buyer must follow. In fact, your waitress works twice as hard when you aren't happy with your meal in order to provide good service. You will do the same as a seller with someone who complains.

Scenario #1

Buyer claims a purchase was not authorized and files a claim through eBay/Credit Card/PayPal after 45+ days. PayPal notifies you and the buyer messages you that they received (or did not receive) an item that someone other than them ordered and it was not authorized.

Emotional Initial Reaction:

You immediately think the buyer is lying...after all, they got the item...you have delivery tracking, but they didn't know it was ordered or who ordered it? Yeah, right....they have buyer's remorse and want their money back, or they borrowed it for the time they needed it and they no longer need it and want their money back, or they broke it.

Rational Calm Thought Process:

(a) This person may be sick, mentally challenged, or elderly and has forgotten.

(b) The buyer reviewed their credit card statement and could not figure out what in the world they ordered from "uselessstuff". They don't recognize that store name, and 2 months have passed.

(c) Their spouse ordered something with the card that they were unaware of.

(d) Their card may have been charged twice for the transaction. Always go look at your account to assure that has not happened as a "first check", as well as checking tracking on the item to assure it has delivery confirmation.

(e) Check to see if you received good feedback from them, which you can report back to them and to eBay/PayPal.

(f) Buyer is experiencing credit card fraud/identify theft/account hacked. Many times an identity thief will use a credit card number or hacked account to purchase a small dollar transaction to see if the transaction will successfully go through. If it does, then they move on to the $900 new iPhone and have it shipped to a different rented "Mailboxes-R-Us" location.

(g) The buyer is lying.

Despite the reason, your first response to the buyer should be one of empathy. Assume they are truly in a position where they did not order that item and just realized they were charged for it on their credit card when they reviewed a statement. Put yourself in their shoes. You would be confused, afraid of fraud, concerned that you are beginning to forget things if you are elderly, etc., etc. A simple note like the following *(do not include what is in small black italic bold print, this is info for you explaining what the purpose of the verbiage is)* of:

"Thank you for making me aware of this situation. I am so sorry that you are experiencing problems with your credit card

> **(this puts the responsibility/problem with the card company and/or eBay/PayPal, not with you or your item).**

I'm certain that eBay will work diligently with you to resolve this issue

> **(takes the responsibility to handle the situation out of your hands).**

For your convenience, I am attaching a screen shot of the tracking for this item for your easy reference to dates of shipping and receipt confirmation

> **(shows that they did get the item, which is the thing that completes your responsibility as a seller, as well as a link to the original item listing, which may remind them of the purchase).**

In the meantime, if you have the item, please do not return it. eBay/PayPal will send instructions of how to best handle the situation when they complete their investigation. I would not want you to spend unnecessary postage costs and, per rules on returns, I may then be unable to refund or return the item to you at my expense, depending upon the outcome of their investigation.

> **(lets them know that just because they send something back that you are not automatically obligated to refund and again, puts the responsibility on PayPal for the rules).**

I hope this situation is quickly resolved for you, and if I can provide any additional information that you may feel would be helpful, please feel free to message me. Best of luck."

Even if they are actually lying, it shows that you have your ducks in a row and are prepared for whatever they have in mind. If they are not lying, this provides a great deal of empathy and understanding for their situation. You have obviously fulfilled your side of the transaction, so this one is easy to prove. When you are notified that the investigation is over, respond with another short note of,

"I just wanted to let you know how sorry I am that you experienced this issue. I can only imagine how frightening it is to know that someone compromised your security. I hope you were able to resolve and reverse the damages by the thief, and wish you my best for a successful and safe resolve".

If you believe them to be a liar, report them to eBay and block them from bidding on your future listings. Either way, they will be hesitant to leave bad feedback. After all, you were so nice to them! If they do leave bad feedback, you can have it removed because the investigation was found in your favor not to be fraudulent.

Seller protection is there to protect you from chargebacks and unauthorized transactions. You never have the opportunity to confirm the credit card....that is eBay's job, and if they fail in their job, they will owe both you and the buyer the money back, but ONLY if you shipped to a confirmed address. Check the address each and every time when printing a label that the term "eligible for seller protection" appears above the buyer's name & address section. If you change one tiny thing within the address that the buyer entered, you lose your protection. eBay seller protection is there to protect you and your reputation against lying buyers, who abuse the return system.

Scenario #2

Buyer requests return and you accept. Buyer returns the item in bad condition, with parts missing, or sends a totally different item altogether.

Emotional Initial Reaction:

That ^%$#&^&*!!!! They're trying to rip me off. Now I'm going to have to refund them and I have a piece of ^%$# that I can't resell!! I've lost $$$$.

Rational Calm Thought Process:

(a) EBay has rules/processes in place to protect me.

(b) I have good photos of the item before it was sent and (may have) recorded serial numbers and/or had a security tag on the item.

(c) My security policies and return policies are strong.

(d) Perhaps the buyer sent back the wrong item by mistake.

(e) The buyer opened a case for the wrong item/seller.

(f) The buyer is a thief.

Do not refund. Contact eBay immediately. They will most likely tell you to contact the buyer to try to work it out, but at least they now have notes that you know the item returned was either misused, is the wrong item, or is not in the same condition as received. Send a message to the buyer that says *(do not include what is shown in small black italic bold lettering; this is info for you explaining what the purpose of the verbiage is)*:

Good morning/afternoon. I wanted to let you know that I received your return package, but the item inside is not in the same condition as when it was sent

(or has missing parts, is not the same item, etc.)

It appears that perhaps you mistakenly put the wrong item into the box or perhaps confused me with another seller.

(this gives the buyer an "out" since you caught them and now eBay knows it, too).

I have attached photos of the condition of the item when shipped, as shown in the listing; along with additional date stamped photos of the item I took that were not in the listing, as well as photos of the condition of the item you returned.

(My phone camera shows the date taken briefly when the photo is opened, at which time I can take a screen shot to send. You can google how to do this on your particular phone model and whether this option is available to you. This definitively shows condition prior to sending in case one of your "extra" photos is needed, and provides photos of the returned item condition that eBay can now see).

I also included a security tag (or security mark, etc.) on this item which is no longer present

(if you did this and provide photos of tag on item).

Per eBay's return policies on the item being in same condition, I am unable to issue a refund.

(puts the rules for a return back on eBay).

I include their return policies within my terms and conditions in the listing, and unfortunately, the item you sent is not a qualifying return

(lets the buyer know you are not folding as the easy victim they want you to be).

Please review the attached photos and check to assure that the correct item was sent, or that you did not confuse me with another seller.

(Again, gives them an opportunity to admit to a "mistake").

I feel sure this was an error and I will be happy to return this item to you if you desire, with postage prepaid by you. I look forward to hearing from you regarding this, and will work closely with eBay throughout this dispute so that we both follow proper protocol, which helps avoid the penalties associated with abuse of buyer/seller protection policies with eBay, or even worse, possible felony criminal penalties from the postal service for what they may deem as a fraudulent insurance claim of damages since your statement of damage is used

(reminds them of consequences of fraud).

I have already spoken with eBay, who will be monitoring our communication, and encourage you to do the same if you feel there is an error. I was advised by them to attempt to work out a resolution with you prior to escalating the case

(gives them an opportunity to cancel the case without eBay getting involved....remember, thieves don't want to be caught and want you to easily give up).

Thank you for your time and understanding of my position. I await your response."

9 times out of 10, this case will go away. If not, and you get a response, it also offers opportunity for the buyer to slip up in their response to you. They are going to be angry that you caught them, and in that anger, they may slip and say "it's the same item, I just used it a couple of times and didn't like how it worked", or "I forgot to put the xxxx back in the box when I sent it to you", or "it was cheap, I barely banged it and it broke!" or best of all "I'm going to leave you bad feedback if you don't refund!". Any of those responses verifies that it is not in the "same condition" and the last one is considered "feedback extortion" by eBay, and you can point eBay to the communication and they will immediately close the case in your favor. If the buyer then leaves bad feedback, you can have it removed and the buyer cannot reopen the case.

If they do not respond to your message within a couple of days, you can call eBay back for advice, and ask for the fraud department so you get a trained representative. They will be able to review pictures and communication and may choose to immediately close the case, or will further advise you. If time expires and the buyer hasn't responded, eBay should close the case in your favor, but don't count on it. If they do not close the case, or find in favor of the buyer, contact eBay and ask for a Dispute specialist, while calmly pointing to all of your evidence for reconsideration. Do not give up on this. Dispute a 2nd time, if necessary…disputing with different representatives often ends in different results. If the item is over $500 in value, ask for a "high value" representative. They have much better training and knowledge and handle high-end item disputes on a regular basis, and can actually make decisions for reversal and money refunded to you. The "eBay for Business" facebook page is also a great resource for assistance from knowledgeable eBay employees.

There is no way to address every scenario you will face. The most important parts to remember are:

- Don't admit or indicate guilt on your part.
- Don't cave to someone you suspect of lying.
- Empathize and treat even the thief with respect and professionalism and communicate with the assumption of innocence, but protect yourself in your language used by gently reminding them of policies and/or the arsenal of weapons they didn't realize you had, as well as terms written within your listings.
- Give the buyer an "out" on their attempt at fraud so they can save face, or perhaps they slip up and say something that resolves a case in your favor.
- Communicate with eBay first, and if the buyer is unreasonable/abusive in their communication, don't respond to the buyer, contact eBay and let them handle it. Walk away and calm down before action, don't take things personally, and work with rational thinking, not emotion.
- Check the feedback of that buyer, as well as feedback left for other sellers for code words that indicate this may be a pattern, and point out that behavior to eBay. You would be surprised at how often eBay does not check that info for past behavior history of a bad buyer.
- Report every buyer you suspect of lying/abuse of policy to eBay and point them to any suspect feedback language you find.
- Immediately block any buyer you suspect of fraud.

You will not do yourself, nor other sellers, any favors by just rolling over and accepting a fraudulent return. It encourages the thieves to continue their abuse, and encourages the spread of the practice. You never know when your report of a fraudulent buyer may be the final straw that gets them eliminated from eBay. EBay takes pride in claiming to be a "Safe Marketplace". Whether it feels like it at times or not, those safety measures are also there for you, as a seller. You just have to be prepared, know the rules better than the eBay employee and the buyer, and protect yourself within your listings in order to successfully fight for that protection. Of course, each situation will require the decision by you as to whether it's worth fighting. If it's a $10 item, you may just choose to refund the buyer without a return and begrudgingly move on. As stated previously, you get discounts for not having strikes on your account. I would hate to lose an escalated case over a $10 item that ends up costing me a $100 discount at the end of the month on my fees. Regardless of how you decide to handle the situation, report the buyer for abuse of the return system.

CHAPTER 9

Packaging and Shipping,

or "The Space and Time (and Cost) Continuum"

You know those people who love to gift wrap and take joy in putting things into boxes, taping, wrapping, etc.? Yeah, I don't like those people. My least favorite thing about selling online is packing and shipping. Buying the item is fun, researching is fun, photographing/writing the description doesn't make me mad, watching the item end on auction or receiving that little "cha-ching" (yes, the eBay phone app alerts you by a cash register sound when an item sells) on your phone is absolutely the best part because you've made money....but shipping...ugh.

SPACE REQUIREMENTS

Not only are supplies expensive and in constant need of checking/replacing stock, you need to have a space to store it all, and there will be more of it than you ever realized. Finding an area where you can store quantities of flat boxes, bubble wrap, peanuts, packaging paper, etc., while still having your ruler, postal scale, tape, scissors, box cutter handy was my biggest challenge. As much as I hated it, in my prior home, I finally just gave in and turned my formal dining area into my "photography & pack/ship area. It was part of the first room you saw when the front door was opened, but was my only choice in a home where I didn't want to have to climb stairs and carry stuff up & down them on a regular basis. If you're young, perhaps that will work for you. At my age, my knees & ankles scream enough at me under my own weight, without adding 40 pounds of packages & trying to balance everything while a small dog tries to murder me via tripping.

Before dedicating a space for all of this, I found myself constantly setting up and taking down my photo booth & lights, trying to store boxes in the garage, which (because of a home remodel and stored materials, along with my husband's tools) was just as much a tripping hazard as the dog/stairs combination with an obstacle course added. I would hide the postal scale in a kitchen cabinet, along with the tape, scissors, tape measure, box cutter in a junk drawer, packing paper stuffed into the pantry, etc., and then run back and forth from place to place to package an item. Just give in….you may think you can hide it all, but unless you have a spare room that is virtually unused in your home, it's impossible to do. It was easier for me to say "excuse the dining area…I'm an eBay seller", than to waste time doing all of the above. I had storage units, but electricity, printing capabilities, and the Vegas climate were prohibitive for me to work there. You may find a place where you can make it work, but most of us are stuck having to use our homes. Thankfully, we recently moved into a different home, and I now have a 500 sf air-conditioned converted garage area for my business, which has made a world of difference in both productivity and presentation and a stress-free living environment, as well as saving the monthly cost of storage units.

PLANNING FOR COSTS

You will need to keep accurate records of your expenses, not only for tax purposes, but also for calculating what shipping a typical package will cost you. Boxes (with the exception of priority boxes that you get for free), will cost you between 40 cents to $15 each, depending upon your need. Bubble wrap is about $20 for a decent size roll; tape is close to $20 for an 8 pack. Packaging paper is about $1.00/pound. It adds up quickly and you need to be able to determine what to add to the cost of an item to cover your expenses. My average cost for packaging is just over $3.00/item. If you sell shirts, your cost may be only 30 cents. If you sell glassware or china, it will be much more. If I can add $3.00 to the cost of each item sold, my expenses are covered when the items sells. You may choose to list the item with a flat rate shipping cost that is more than actual costs by a couple of bucks instead. I find that buyers don't like high postage, and eBay allows buyers to star-rate you on shipping costs, but many people find success in doing it that way, so go for it if it works for you! My personal preference is to just build it into my pricing, spread out over every item.

For accounting purposes, there are multiple programs available, but the least expensive and easiest to use for me was a software called "Easy Auctions Tracker", that was less than $60 annually. Unfortunately, eBay ended their partnership with them when they began handling their own payments. EBay's reports are decent if you keep good notes. If you have basic spreadsheet skills, just use Excel, keep the eBay reports in a file and just enter basic totals from their reports. I find that is better for me than an actual accounting program and the time-consuming task of entering everything. I just set up a separate page to enter expenses. Your tax professional may be able to recommend a good inventory software for your particular needs. I know many who use GoDaddy, which downloads into Quickbooks, but I've never used it. Most have free trials to make it easy to try out before investing in your software. Unless you're selling more than a few items a week, I don't find anything more than a spreadsheet necessary.

WAIT, DID YOU SAY FREE BOXES?

Yes, you can order free boxes for Priority Mail and Priority Mail Express packages from USPS. They have a variety of sizes/options if you use Priority Mail. I use more Priority flat rate padded envelopes and Priority small flat rate boxes than any other supply...and they're free. Not only are they free, they are delivered to your door free of charge! It's hard to beat that deal. You can also pick up the boxes at your local post office, but the variety or size you need may or may not be available. Just order them in all sizes to keep on hand from the USPS website.

The catch? Priority mail is a bit more expensive than standard class postage in most cases, so buyers sometimes pay a bit more in shipping. It is typically 3-day shipping time, though, so there's an upside. The boxes are given as an incentive for people to use Priority Mail. This means that there are restrictions and you have to agree that you will use those supplies ONLY for Priority mail purposes. You cannot use them to ship first class, or use them to ship with other carriers, like FedEx or UPS. Don't use their bubble mailers as packing materials, etc. They are given to you for free for use with priority mail only, period. Don't abuse the gift, or those supplies will go away if people take advantage. You used to get free Priority mail tape, but USPS found that people were using it for everything, and now it's no longer available without jumping through hoops for it. It was great tape, too......bastards.

If you decide to purchase a "store" subscription from eBay when you reach a fairly high level of listings, eBay also offers some free shipping supplies quarterly to store owners. The amount is based on your store level.

CALCULATING SHIPPING IN YOUR LISTING

Don't guess. Weigh the item, unless you know it will fit into a Priority Flat Rate envelope/box and you plan to use that. The differences in cost of shipping will vary greatly from item to item in most cases. Again, if you're selling the same item over and over again, this will be easier for you, but if you're like me and may sell a tiny ring, and then a 50 pound set of china, you will not want to wing it because you will short yourself more often than not.

Boxes and packaging materials weigh more than you think. A large size box can weigh 2 pounds alone, and then add several sheets of packing paper and you can add 4 pounds to an item's weight pretty quickly. You will get an idea over time as to how much weight to add to an item in order to accommodate packaged weight, but it never hurts to just weigh the box and a handful of packing paper until you are comfortable in estimating weight. I typically add 1 pound for smaller items that require padding, 2 pounds for items that require up to a 12" square box size to package, and 4 pounds for large items. 5-7 pounds is added if double boxing a fragile item will be required, depending upon size of the outer box needed.

Extremely important: Familiarize yourself with what each carrier considers to be "oversize". It can make a shipment go from $35 to $300 in a hurry. Measure carefully and round up to the next inch of your box size, because that's how the carriers calculate. My rule of thumb is not to buy anything that will end up being "oversize". No one will pay that kind of shipping cost. If you choose to freight large appliances as your line of business, all my best to you but I, personally, will rarely sell anything large unless there is a

LOT of profit in the item and if I can have someone else handle the shipping.

When you list, check out the different options on the postage calculator. You can offer more than one option to your buyer, but I typically list the cheapest as the first choice, because that is what the buyer sees. There are times that I will not offer anything other than Priority shipping. Priority mail is handled for 3 days. FedEx Smart post can take up to 9 days for delivery. The longer a package is handled by the carrier, the more of an opportunity they have to destroy it….which I believe is actually a challenge to them at times. Extremely fragile smaller items go Priority mail, period. International shipments go Priority mail, period. Other types of international shipping may not provide good tracking or delivery confirmation, both of which are important for your protection. If the international buyer doesn't want to pay for Priority shipping, then don't buy my item, because I'm not going to lose the cost of shipping and the cost of the item if it gets lost or broken along the way, especially considering that shipping can easily be in excess of $50 for a small item.
The only exception I will make to that is if the item is a very low dollar, small item and is not fragile…then I may choose first class.

Packages up to 70 pounds are processed on conveyor belts and packages are dropped up to 15' into bins at carrier facilities, where your fragile china plate may land in bottom and have a 70 pound set of weights dropped onto it. It needs to packed well enough to survive that.

If you are going to offer international shipping, also be very aware of what may be restricted to send to other Countries. Many times, precious metals and gemstones are restricted and are only covered against loss if you use a certain service. Priority Mail Express, where postage is 2 or more times the cost of regular Priority shipping can end up being the only true "trackable" option on some items. If you specify regular priority and find out later that you need Priority Express to be protected in case of loss or damage, you will eat a good chunk of money or will be forced to cancel the transaction due to "problems with the buyer's address". It isn't a strike against your seller account if you do that, but it is a disappointment to the buyer and a loss of a sale to you, just because you didn't do your homework ahead of time. You can also choose to use eBay's International Shipping Program, where you ship the item to their warehouse address, and they forward to the buyer, which takes all responsibility for shipping issues off of you. The drawback? Shipping becomes significantly more expensive for international buyers, who may then choose to skip your item due to that cost of shipping, although many sellers find success and peace of mind using that service. Buyers are always responsible for import fees/taxes/duties for their Country. Some international buyers may try to fool you into thinking you're responsible for them after a sale.

Side Note: For shipments to Alaska, Hawaii & US Territories, such as the Virgin Islands, be aware that these locations may significantly increase your cost to ship if you offer free or flat-rate shipping. Make sure you choose the option in the shipping section of your listing to add an amount to cover that extra cost.

TOP 3 CARRIERS PROS & CONS:

USPS: My favorite.

Pros: They're quick, reliable, trackable and they more easily pay insurance claims for the most part on values under $100. You can choose media mail for books and certain other items and pay a very low rate for a very heavy box. Priority mail comes with a minimum of $100 free insurance coverage, and you get free boxes with Priority Mail.

Cons: Cost on some packages can be prohibitive. When you arrange pickup, it's almost always "next day" pickup and pickup is not available in all areas. You have to package your item quickly or make a trip to the Post Office to meet your handling time. Remember that the package must be scanned and accepted to meet shipping requirements, so where eBay tells you have until midnight to ship, you really only have until your post office closes.

FEDEX:

Pros: They're cheaper on larger and heavier items. Pickup can occur with as little as 24 hours' notice for everything (based on availability in your area) other than "Smart Post", which requires that you drop off a package. There are costs for pickup. $100 insurance is provided free.

Cons: They're slower in most cases, and they will almost always initially reject every insurance claim unless they package the item. You will have to be prepared with photos of your packaging technique to show that you have followed their guidelines for packaging. Familiarize yourself with those guidelines. They are rough on packages, so package extra well if the item is the least bit fragile. Buyers report that outer boxes are often damaged and are surprised to see contents in one piece. Your postage calculated on eBay is an "estimate" in FedEx's eyes. You may be charged more if your weight/dimensions are not accurate, or if their machine messes up, and you then have a fight to get the shipping reduced. Always round up to the next 1" and 1 pound increment when using FedEx if you are even a small fraction over, because that's what they do.

UPS:

Pros: They're cheaper on larger on heavier items than USPS. Pickup can occur with as little as 24 hours' notice for a fee. They are more careful than other "ground" ship companies in my past experience. Buyers report that packages are typically in decent condition when they arrive.

Cons: They're slower in most cases than USPS and FedEx, and they too, will reject every insurance claim (according to my pack & ship place...no personal experience), so take the same precautions as with FedEx. UPS is also a "Dimensional Weight" shipper (which will be addressed in the next chapter)..

PROFESSIONAL PACKAGING SERVICES

I do occasionally use a professional packaging service. It's expensive because you are paying a premium on both the materials and the time it takes for them to do the work. However, on certain items, especially very fragile, high dollar items, it is well worth the cost. I recently sold a 50-piece set of fragile, stoneware dishes. They were worth a good bit of money, with that set selling on a regular basis for $600 with $200+ shipping added. I paid $75 for the set, so I had some room to factor in professional packaging. I listed the set for $600 with $150 shipping, with a $300 discount if someone did local pickup. I paid $315 for the packaging and shipping of the 3 double-boxed, fully wrapped & insured packages...as you can see, I rolled a portion of the shipping costs into the item price. eBay buyers will willingly pay more for an item, but balk at extremely high shipping costs. I weighed and sent photos to the packaging service for an estimate, which they will honor for 6 months. It still left me with a great profit margin, and one of the benefits of using a professional packaging company is that if the item is insured and it breaks, and the carrier refuses the claim, the professional packaging company then pays you the declared value. Any time that foam core wrapping is needed for a heavy, fragile item that sells for a high dollar amount, especially if I paid very little for it, I use a professional packaging company...believe me, you do not want to cut foam core in your house and deal with what you would swear was an explosion of an electrically charged, static-filled bean bag. Yes, I could have shipped and packaged myself for less, but it would have taken me 4 hours, I would have been sweating, cussing and had an aching back, and then worried about whether I would be paid if it was damaged in shipping. That extra cost becomes a small cost if you bought right in the beginning and properly plan in your pricing.

You will find that over time, you will develop a "sixth sense" about how to ship each item, but always check eBay's postage calculator for the best option, with these items considered:

1. Value of the item
2. Whether the item is fragile
3. Size of the item
4. Weight of the Item
5. Speed that it needs to arrive – with special Consideration given around holidays.
6. Restrictions for international shipping
7. Customer's desire of time vs. value – offer multiple Shipping options.

CHAPTER 10
FedEx and UPS Surprise Charges
Planning and Avoiding excessive "Dimensional Weight" costs

Sellers have mentioned "surprise" charges on their postage costs through FedEx and UPS. The situation is that you calculate postage at one amount, and suddenly you are charged at a much different cost than estimated. Take "Dimensional Weight" into consideration, which means you can get dinged with some hefty surprise costs....costs that you have almost zero chance of arguing, because eBay is the carrier's customer, not you. You will notice when printing FedEx postage that eBay warns you that the amount they quote is an estimated amount and actual charges may differ. Remember that eBay, for example, may offer you a 40% discount over full retail, but they are getting a 50% discount from these carriers, so eBay is making money from the shipping you pay, as well, which means that eBay has their own interests at heart when it comes to arguing these charges. Good luck taking money out of their pocket.

What is "Dimensional Weight", you ask? FedEx/UPS and now UPSP charges, based on the amount of cubic feet your package takes up in their trucks/planes (dimensions). You could ship a beach ball that requires a 24"x24"x24" box, which weighs only 3 pounds. However, the "dimensional weight" of that package is 84 pounds, because it takes up 8 cubic feet of space. You will be charged as though the package weighs 84 pounds! Dimensional weight comes into play on every package. Keep a close eye on your eBay invoice for FedEx/UPS charges, which do not show up until days after the package is delivered. You are not immediately charged because they want to verify that the information you entered is correct. ALWAYS round up to the next inch and to the next pound increment if you are even a fraction of an amount over. If you are wrong, you will be billed full retail price for the shipment and will lose the significant discount recognized through eBay's postage system.

You should also be aware that if you purchase, i.e., a 12"x12"x12" box, the measurement printed on the box is the INTERIOR dimensions of the box, not the EXTERIOR dimensions, so your postage will be calculated by shippers at a 13"x13"x13" rate. Make sure you enter the correct dimensions for the exterior of the box, not the size marked on it. Otherwise, this could lead to a "postage due" invoice to your buyer or unexpected charges to you on your eBay invoice, which is never a good thing.

How do I avoid the surprise charges? There are ways to help assure you calculate and are charged correctly:

1. eBay's postage calculator now calculates the DIM weight on their site. I always double check, though, using this calculation on domestic packages: LxWxH/166 or this calculation on international shipments: LxWxH/139. That would mean that if you have a package that is 12" x 12" x 30" then that is 12x12x30 = 4230 divided by 166, which is a Dimensional weight of 26 pounds. You can also use this to calculate the proper dimensional weight of your package if using FedEx/UPS, and enter that weight as the shipping weight of your item when listing. There is an online calculator to help determine dimensional weight at www.shippingeasy.com. Remember to round up to the next inch when measuring if the box goes over by even the tiniest amount.

2. Familiarize yourself with what "oversize" means to each carrier. It's a combination of the length, width and depth of a package. If you go over a certain number of inches, your postage costs increase dramatically. If you're close to that number, you will want to adjust your box size down if at all possible, or even begin to avoid purchases that you know will exceed that size once packaged. Sometimes a one inch difference on one of the dimensions can make a significant difference in postage cost.

3. Many people open a free FedEx & UPS account and do print postage for FedEx/UPS packages there instead of through eBay. You will have to associate a credit/debit card to the account unless you go through applying for a credit account with them, where you are billed monthly. The calculators on their own website account for dimensional weight. Where eBay has now taken that into consideration, they do have glitches in their system on occasion. Remember, if printed through eBay, eBay is their customer and they will barely speak to you, leaving you to argue with eBay, who will then point to FedEx/UPS as the problem. Don't forget to manually upload tracking info into eBay when you print postage outside of their system, though.

Yes, you will lose that discount that eBay offers for printing through their website. However, with FedEx & UPS, when I opened my account (which I tied to my PayPal debit card for easy expense tracking), I had a sales representative contact me within 2 days from each of the companies to discuss the volume of shipping I would be doing. They want your business. When they call, tell them that you use their service as often as possible, and that you ship 20+ items/week. That seems to be the magic number. Let them know that you use a variety of shippers, based on cost, but prefer them because of convenience, and that you are an eBay seller.

They will want you to ship all 20 packages with them, and will give you the "eBay seller" discount, which is almost equivalent to eBay's discount that you are given. I actually only ship about 2-3 boxes per week with FedEx, but my discount has remained.

4. I have heard many sellers talk about how they underestimate the size/weight of a package to save on postage or use Media Mail rates for things that do not qualify. Do not be one of these people. Different postal facilities have different equipment and many packages are now automatically weighed and measured by cameras. Postal services can even sometimes provide and research photos of condition of your particular package along the transit route. Their machines will eventually catch you underestimating size/weight. There are consequences for that behavior, including being retroactively charged for full retail postage (meaning if you typically receive a 25%-75% discount through eBay, you will then be charged full price). Your buyer could receive a "postage due" notice on the package, which will assure bad feedback, or the package being refused. If you are caught doing this over and over (not just a one-time error), eBay can suspend your account. Ebay and USPS have an agreement to automatically both underpaid and overpaid postage, so with USPS, you will not often get away with the behavior. You can find any postage differences by checking your eBay account for Shipping Cost Adjustments. Fedex and UPS do not charge postage until after the package is delivered, so you will assure that you pay much more than estimated if you try it with them. Some offenses could result in a felony charge of postal fraud and cost you up to 5 years in prison and up to $250,000 in fines. It's a serious crime with serious consequences. Just be an honest person.

CHAPTER 11

Accounting/Record Keeping

An important part of any business venture is good record keeping. It can consume a good bit of your time if you are not organized. I will not give accounting advice in this section except that a good CPA or Enrolled Agent is worth their weight in gold and will more than pay for their cost in savings recognized.

A home-based business (or any business) can recognize multiple tax benefits and with tax law changes, you will most likely need someone knowledgeable to assure you are in compliance with your local, state and federal tax and business laws, and if you decide to incorporate, they can help determine the best type of business for your needs, whether it be a partnership, LLC, C-Corp, etc., or whether you qualify for hobby income, based on how you treat it.

There are many online accounting programs you can use. Some of the more common ones are QuickBooks, Go Daddy Bookkeeping, etc. Most all have demos and trial versions of each for you to try to determine which may be best for you. Since I like the spreadsheet format and since it allows tying my inventory and purchase cost to individual sales for eBay, I chose that method. I cannot stress the importance enough for keeping accurate and organized records of your inventory, purchase costs, supplies costs, fees, sales prices, refunds, losses, mileage, etc. (check with a CPA for a list of everything you need to track). Any of the programs above will help alleviate much of the burden of manually tracking.

With a new law passed in 2021, online payment services such as eBay's managed payments, PayPal, Venmo, Apple Pay, Cash App, etc., are now required, by law, to issue a 1099 for transactions equaling over $600 total for the year. Regardless of whether you get a 1099 or not, you are responsible for reporting income tax for even $1 made in online sales according to the IRS, with the exception of selling your own personally owned items...and even then, you need proof of a loss, such as original receipt for the item, etc. Also be aware that part of that banking law requires financial institutions to report any regular cash transactions of certain levels to the IRS. So if you sell on marketplace and begin depositing cash on a regular basis, it could trigger an audit. If you decide to leave the IRS out of your cash business, you're taking your own risks.

It may be easy enough with low-volume sales to keep everything in a spreadsheet. Once you hit a higher volume or higher dollar, you may be shocked at how much time and energy it takes to track everything. It will then be time to get serious and get a program to streamline the process. You will want to do the same if you begin to find yourself struggling to keep up. You make money when listing, not doing paperwork.

Be aware that you cannot wait an entire year and then decide to buy a program & download information from eBay. eBay keeps much of the information for only 90 days, other than yearly reporting info. Your detail on items and ability to download eBay fees to an outside tracking software, etc. is lost after 90 days, so keep on top of this task.

Keep receipts! If you buy something at a garage sale, notate the address, description & amount paid on a slip of paper, at a minimum. Keep receipts for supplies purchases. Keep a mileage log for any business-related drive. If you work from home, keep a record of your power costs, space used, telephone, internet, utilities, etc. A dedicated debit or credit card will be a huge help in this. Number your inventory items and keep a detailed description of each item. "Blue plate", as a description, will not work to easily track things if you end up with 15 blue plates after 5 years of buying inventory. I spend about 2 hours weekly on bookkeeping. It's not hard if you have a good system, a good program and are disciplined, and I can turn one report over to my CPA at tax time.

CHAPTER 12

Quick Reference - FAQ
Top 10 Most Common Questions and how to Address Them

I've covered some of these scenarios previously and provided answers, but wanted to add to the list and consolidate the top questions that I hear into one area for quick reference of responses, if needed. Be sure to thoroughly read the responses in quotation marks, as you will need to customize for your situation in certain places.

Question 1: **A buyer sent a message saying that even though a package shows as "delivered", they have not received it. How do I respond? What do I need to do?**

Answer: Your job as a seller is done at that point. An insurance claim cannot be filed on a delivered package. There is really nothing you can, or need to do, except provide good customer service, which can be done while protecting yourself at the same time with 2 simples steps:

What to do:

- Call eBay and point them to the buyer's message/case (if opened). If a case has been opened by the buyer, eBay should immediately close it in your favor immediately, and will contact the buyer themselves. This assures that if the buyer chooses to leave bad feedback, you can get it removed.

- Send the buyer a message that says,

    "Thank you for contacting me regarding this package. I am so sorry that you are experiencing issues with locating the delivered package. I did double check, and it is showing as "delivered" via tracking. For a lost package, eBay will typically ask you to check with neighbors and other family members who may have picked up the package, or had it mis-delivered to their home. Also check with your local post office so that they can ask the carrier, who may remember the package itself. Unfortunately, because postage is printed through eBay's system and it shows as "delivered", the extent of my ability to assist within eBay's system ends at the point of delivery. Please contact both your local post office, as well as eBay for their guidance in helping to locate the package, and please let me know the results. I am always worried, as well as disappointed, when either the postal service or a thief interferes with your receipt of an item. I wish you all the best in locating it. Please let me know if I can be of any assistance in providing tracking information or package information."

This will show empathy, point them to where they can get assistance, and takes the burden off of you for the responsibility to assist in something where your job is done.

Question #2: A Buyer (after purchase) asked me to ship to an alternate address. Should I do this?

Answer/What to do: It's up to you, but be aware that while eBay will cover you as long as the request is done through eBay messaging, the credit card company/PayPal will not, and the buyer can file a claim with PayPal for up to 180 days after delivery. If it's an item you can afford to lose and the buyer has great feedback, you are probably fine, but if there is any question, then don't do it and send a message that says,

"Thank you for contacting me prior to shipping the package. However, I am unable to ship to any address other than what is a "confirmed" address, as doing so is outside of the buyer/seller protection policies that are in place to protect us both in this transaction. I can either ship to the address on file, or I can cancel the transaction, and you can repurchase, and assure that you change to the alternate address via eBay's system as the "ship to" address prior to checkout. Please let me know which you prefer, and I will be happy to accommodate."

Is there a chance that the buyer will tell you to cancel and then never repurchase? Yes...if they were planning to rip you off. Someone who is legitimate will follow through with one of the choices you provide. If the buyer does not answer, cancel the transaction for reason of "problem with buyer's address" prior to your stated shipping time, so that you do not receive a defect for late shipment and follow up with eBay to assure that you have not received a defect on your account because you did not ship on time. You would think eBay's system would automatically see that the transaction was cancelled, but I have found a defect registered for late shipping on an item where I had to cancel. eBay will not remove defects if you let more than 90 days pass. You can either call them or use the "appeal a defect" option on their website.

Question #3: Can I use a Priority Flat Rate Box for regular Priority Mail if I cover up the words "Flat Rate"? Can I cut a flat rate box to fit the item and ship regular Priority Mail?

Answer: No. There used to be an exception that if you paid the regular priority rate, then you could manipulate the box and cover or cut the "flat-rate" marking on the box. The postal service updated that in 2020 to allow only Flat Rate postage to be charged for Flat Rate packaging. Also, be aware that flat rate packaging will allow the packaging to "bulge", but the package must be closed "within the normal folds", meaning that, you cannot, i.e., leave one end of the container open and seal it with additional cardboard/tape to ship an item that is longer than the natural fold of the box.

Question #4: I sent a package, and it is showing as received by the Post Office, but seems stuck and has not been delivered, and it's been more than ample time to have arrived. The buyer is getting concerned and sent a message and/or opened an "item not received" case. What do I do?

Answer/What to do: go to www.usps.com and file a claim on the package. The process is simple and normally a claim will result in finding the package. If not, it will force the package to be declared "lost", and you can then collect an insurance claim without question. Unfortunately, if the package is not insured, you are the one who will suffer the loss, not the buyer.

After the inquiry is filed with the carrier, send a message to the buyer of

"Thank you for bringing this situation to my attention. I am so sorry there is an issue with the postal service on your package. The package was shipped on mm/dd/yy, but as you mentioned, tracking is not showing the progress as it should. I have opened a case with the postal service, and am awaiting their response as to whether they can locate and deliver the package successfully, or whether they will declare it as lost, at which time I will issue an immediate refund of your purchase price and any shipping paid. I will be in touch with you as I hear back from them with updates. Rest assured that I am as concerned as you and will stay on top of

the situation. Again, thank you for your notification and your patience while the postal service completes their investigation."

Also immediately contact eBay. You have only 3 business days to respond to an open case on eBay, or that case will be automatically closed in favor of the buyer and they will be refunded. That means that even if the package is then received on day 4, you have no recourse and have then lost money and the item, and all you can hope is that the buyer returns the item or repays you for it (which is virtually impossible for them to do through eBay's system). You will also not be reimbursed by any postal insurance you purchased because the item was delivered. It is imperative that you contact eBay and have them extend the deadline through escalation of the case. As long as the eBay representative checks tracking, they will see that the item is still in transit and should do so. If the representative is hesitant, hang up and get a different representative. As previously mentioned, some representatives are more knowledgeable than others and it just takes getting the right one at times I had one item that took almost an entire month to make it to Canada. eBay was great about extending the case (they will extend by 7 days in my experience, so you have to call them weekly to get another extension) and the item was eventually found and delivered. Check tracking on the package daily and keep in touch with your buyer throughout the process, as they are going to be extremely concerned that they have not received their item. Just keep assuring them that you are working closely with eBay and the postal service to assure that they either get the item or receive a full refund. If you insured the item, file the claim immediately. I had one package where I was reimbursed by insurance, had refunded the buyer, and the package eventually showed back up on my doorstep after touring the world, with markings from multiple different Countries. I tried to reimburse USPS for the insurance they had paid, but found that to be an impossible task, so I was paid twice once it resold. You will eventually have a package that causes a headache. Just keep in close contact with both eBay and the buyer throughout the process and always protect yourself with insurance for any item that you cannot afford to lose.

Question #5: I have a buyer who hasn't paid for an item. What do I need to do?

Answer/What to do:

- Send an invoice to the buyer with a courtesy note of "just a reminder that this item remains unpaid".
- If no response, open a non-paying bidder case with eBay. You are able to set your own parameters of how long to give a buyer prior to opening a case. I have mine set for 2 days. If they don't pay by then, they most likely are not going to. No other retailer in the world holds an item and gives you 2 days to pay, so I make the time as short as allowed.
- If buyer pays, ship as normal (the case you opened will automatically close once a buyer pays). If they do not pay, keep an eye on the timing and close the case after 4 business days, at which time you will receive your fees back and will be able to relist the item.

Note: You can set your virtual "eBay assistant" (just an option in your settings) to automatically file these actions on your behalf so that you don't manually have to track, and can then blame eBay's "automated system" for the notices/case if a buyer becomes upset that you opened a case against them.

Question #6. A buyer opened a PayPal claim that an item was not received, or that a fraudulent (unauthorized) purchase occurred on their credit card on an item I sold to them. How do I respond?

Answer/What to do:

- Immediately take the following steps:
- (1) Whether you have tracking on the package and that it shows as delivered.
- (2) Did the buyer leave you positive feedback that would prove they received the item?
- (3) Check your eBay account to assure that the customer was not charged twice. It's not a common problem, but does happen.
- (4) Check to make sure that the transaction was "eligible for protection", i.e., you sent to the confirmed address.

If these requirements were met, you are covered by eBay against unauthorized charge claims.

- Respond to eBay immediately with the tracking info on the package. There is a "black hole" between day 120 & 180 when tracking is no longer available online through USPS to prove that a buyer received an item. If online tracking is not available, immediately request it to be pulled from the archives from the Post Office, in writing, through their website or at your local branch. They are able to access archived information. Make sure to let them know that time is of the essence for their response.
- Send this message to the buyer (even if you think they are scamming):

> *"Thank you for making me aware of this situation. I am so sorry that you are experiencing problems with your credit card. I'm certain that eBay will work diligently with you to resolve this issue. For your convenience, I am attaching a screen shot of the tracking for this item for your easy reference to dates of shipping and receipt confirmation, as well as a link to the original item listing. In the meantime, if you have the item, please do not return it. eBay will send instructions of how to best handle the situation when they complete their investigation. I would not want you to spend unnecessary postage costs and, per rules on returns, I may then be unable to refund or return the item to you at my expense, depending upon the outcome of their investigation. I hope this situation is quickly resolved for you, and if I can provide any additional information that you may feel would be helpful, please feel free to message me. Best regards."*

This puts the responsibility on the Credit Card Company/PayPal and on eBay, shows that they did get the item and the link to the item itself may remind them of the purchase, and keeps them from returning something, thinking they may get a refund. It also shows empathy for their situation. Even if they are lying, it lets them know that you have your ducks in a row and are prepared to fight the case. If you can provide tracking that shows the item was received, you should win the case.

Question #7: *An item I sent was damaged in transit. What do I need to do? Do I file an insurance claim or does the buyer file it?*

Answer/What to do:

- Tell the buyer to open a return case (if they are scamming, they will not want to go through eBay and may just be trying to see if you will refund them without a return).

- Ask for photos of the damage, so you can begin an insurance claim. At that time, you can decide whether you want the item returned, or if the photos they provide are enough to satisfy the carrier as proof (make sure to get photos of the box and packing materials, as well as the damage to the item, and ask the buyer to hang on to (or return) everything for the claim. A basic template may look like this:

    "Thank you for notifying me of the damage. Despite packaging well, the post office conveyor belts, etc., can destroy packages, and I cannot apologize enough for your disappointment. I did have the item insured and may not need you to repackage and send back if you would be kind enough to provide the following:
    (1) Multiple photos of the box and the damage to the box
    (2) A photo showing how the item was packaged so that my insurance claim cannot be denied due to "insufficient packaging" showing it meets carrier requirements.
    (3) Multiple photos of the item itself and the damage that occurred.

    Once those photos, which I need for my insurance claim, are received, I will be in a position to better decide whether to have you return the item or keep the item. Please be aware that the postal service, as well as eBay, requires that all items be retained, including the items, the box and all packaging material. Occasionally, the post office will want to personally inspect an item to decide on a claim and to assure that you and I are not colluding to commit postal fraud, which is a felony. I can assure you that you will not be out a dime on the transaction. I will lose the original shipping cost, and do not wish to spend money again to have a broken item returned, so your cooperation is appreciated. Again, my apologies and appreciation for the inconvenience of providing this info and keeping the item/box/packing materials for 30 days so that I may also recoup some of my losses. Upon receipt of the photos and confirmation that you are willing to retain these items, I will let you know if I need the item returned, or will immediately issue a full refund. So sorry for the disappointment. Thank you."

- If you are satisfied that the item was damaged during shipment, immediately refund the buyer.
- File the claim yourself.

A buyer will not have all of the info needed to file a successful claim, it will be rejected and then they will come after you. Always handle your own insurance claims. Do not provide the buyer with info for them to file a claim. You have no way of tracking that, and they can then open a case against you, and you will not be repaid by the carrier because the buyer has already collected on the package.

Question #8: *A buyer returned an item that is not in the same condition/is not the item I sent. Do I have to refund them? What do I do? Can I fight this?*

Answer/What to do: Do not refund. Contact eBay immediately. They will most likely tell you to contact the buyer to try to work it out, but they now have a record of your complaint. Send a message to the buyer of:

"Good morning/afternoon. I wanted to let you know that I received your return package, but the item inside is not in the same condition as when it was sent/has missing parts/is not the same item. It appears that perhaps you mistakenly put the wrong item into the box, or confused me with another seller? I have attached photos of the condition of the item when shipped, as shown in the listing; along with additional

date stamped photos of the item I took that were not in the listing, as well as photos of the condition of the item you returned. (IF YOU DID THIS – INCLUDE) – I also included a security tag on this item which is no longer present.) Per eBay's return policies on the item being in same condition, I am unable to issue a full refund, as noted in the listing regarding "same condition with all inclusions". Unfortunately, the item you sent is not a qualifying return. Please review the attached photos and check to assure that the correct item was sent. I feel sure this was an error and I will be happy to return this item to you if you desire, with postage prepaid by you. I look forward to hearing from you regarding this, and will work closely with eBay throughout this dispute so that we both follow proper protocol, which helps avoid the penalties associated with abuse of buyer/seller protection policies with eBay, or even worse, possible criminal penalties from the postal service for what they may deem as a felony fraudulent insurance claim of damages. I have already spoken with eBay, who will be monitoring our communication, and encourage you to do the same if you feel there is an error. I was advised by them to attempt to work out a resolution with you prior to escalating the case. Thank you for your time and understanding of my position. I await your response."

This gives the buyer an "out" that it may have been an error, it puts the rules for return back onto eBay, lets the buyer know you are not an easy victim, reminds them of the consequences of fraud, and gives them an opportunity to cancel the case without getting eBay involved. A thief wants an easy target and if you don't give up easily, they typically go away. If this person behaves this way on a regular basis, the last thing they want is for eBay to catch on to their scam, because they will lose their account. In the very least, you get a response from them, where they may actually incriminate themselves with an obvious lie, or may threaten you with bad feedback, which will allow you to win the case. Ask for a Dispute specialist when calling eBay and calmly and nicely present your evidence. Don't give up if you don't get a positive response the first time. Call back 2 or 3 times if necessary, as you may get different results.

Question #9: **As long as I print the label within my handling time, I'm OK on my stated handling time, right?**

Answer: No. You used to be able to get away with that and then ship the next day. Now, eBay requires that you not only print and upload tracking info, but that the package shows as received by the carrier within your stated handling time. For example, if you state 1-day handling time, that is considered 1 business day. If purchased on a Monday, you must ship by Tuesday. If purchased on a Friday, you must ship by Monday. If that Monday is a holiday, you must ship by Tuesday. Saturday, Sunday and postal holidays are not considered business days.

Question #10: **A buyer left me unfair bad feedback without even contacting me with a problem. Can I get it removed?**

Answer: It depends upon the circumstances. If a buyer says you were slow to ship, but you have clear tracking/receipt of package showing and you shipped via the method you chose in your listing, you can get it removed. If the buyer was abusive or vulgar/threatening in their comment, you can get it removed. However, if a buyer says that the item was in poor condition, it will depend on whether you can claim what they said is not true as a specific provable thing. If they said the color is wrong, but you sent the same shirt as in the listing, you may be able to get it removed. If they say it was "more worn than expected", that's their opinion and eBay will stand behind them.

You can always contact the buyer and ask them to revise the feedback. You cannot mention that it affects you negatively in eBay's eyes, or that you lose discounts, etc., but you can explain that you would have accepted a refund, and truly thought the condition was acceptable, and feel that given the opportunity, you could have resolved their dissatisfaction with the item.

You can call the buyer for this, if you choose, and if they included a phone number with eBay. Phone numbers are listed below the buyer's address in many cases, or eBay may be able to provide it to you after a sale (you cannot get email info/phone #/address prior to a sale and asking for that violates the "member to member" contact policy and can get your account suspended or revoked). Sometimes when a buyer knows that you are a single mom (or whatever), just trying to make a living or extra money and not some big company, it adds a human touch and it makes it more difficult for the buyer to be mean or nasty. Always follow up a phone call with a message through eBay messaging of **"Thank you for taking my call earlier today. Per our conversation, blah, blah, blah...."** Or you can send them a message such as:

"Hi. I noticed that you left negative feedback for me, and I was a bit shocked and confused. I work very hard to maintain a positive feedback rating and to remain in good standing with eBay, and I pride myself on going above and beyond to assure all of my customers are happy. I offer free returns, and had no idea that you were unhappy with the item. I would appreciate the opportunity to prove my customer service and try to rectify the situation with you, so that you will truly feel that I did not deserve the negative comment. I am never happy if my buyer is not happy and am truly sorry that you felt the item was unacceptable. Is there anything I can do to change your view of me and possibly earn your respect to change the feedback you left? Thank you for your consideration."

It never hurts to ask the customer and eBay if the feedback can be removed/changed. You may get a return, or you may be ignored, and the feedback may or may not end up being revised, but at least you tried. Don't take it personally….there will always be people out there who take joy in misery, and there is nothing you can do to change those people. The problem is with them, not you, and you can always respond to the feedback when all other options are exhausted with something like "Buyer never contacted me. I accept returns & was unaware of issue-Unfair FB". Then every time you look at the response, you can imagine that "FB" does not stand for Feedback, but rather stands for Friggin' Bast$#@ or Friggin' Bi$#@. ☺

ABOUT THE AUTHOR

Leslie/Neon Press (pen name used for protection of online accounts), was born and raised in South Carolina, where a love for antiques and collectibles was instilled in her by her Father, who owned an Antique Shop.

Leslie spent her first 35 years in her birth place, then ventured West to Colorado, where she met her husband, who shares in her passion of antiques and cool old stuff. Leslie & her husband ran an eBay resell business and were also physically located in multiple antique malls in the area, while both working normal 9:00 – 5:00 jobs, based out of a suburb of Denver. Leslie has been an eBay seller for over 20 years.

Leslie has two grown daughters and is a Grandmother of two boys. Leslie and her husband currently reside in Las Vegas, NV.

After working in the construction industry for over 25 years and owning her own construction management and consulting business, Leslie made the move to follow the passion passed down from her Father, and chose to never work another day in her life by doing what she loves… Hunting & reselling the treasures she finds.

www.ingramcontent.com/pod-product-compliance
Lightning Source LLC
Chambersburg PA
CBHW050315230526
45471CB00005B/2194